Agent-Based Computational Economics Using NetLogo

Authored by

Romulus-Catalin Damaceanu

Faculty of Economics
"Petre Andrei" University of Iasi
Romania

CONTENTS

CHAPTER

FOREWORD

The eBook explores the techniques, researchers can create, use and implement multi-agent computational models in Economics by using NetLogo software platform. Problems of economic science can be solved using multi-agent modelling (*MAM*). This technique uses a computer model to simulate the actions and interactions of autonomous entities in a network, for analyzing the effects on the entire economic system. *MAM* combines elements of game theory, complex systems, emergence and evolutionary programming. Monte Carlo method is used to introduce random elements. The models simulate the simultaneous operations of several agents in an attempt to recreate and predict complex economic phenomena. The process is one that starts emerging from the micro to macroeconomic level. Individual agents are presumed to act in what they perceive as their own interest such as reproduction, economic benefit, social status, provided that their awareness is limited.

NetLogo is a software platform designed by Uri Wilensky in the year 1999. NetLogo is in the process of development and modernization in the frame of Centre for Connected Learning and Computer-Based Modelling - Northwestern University, Illinois, USA. NetLogo is written in Java language and can be run on all major platforms (Windows, Mac, Linux *etc.*). In addition, individual models can be run as Java applets inside web pages. NetLogo is freeware and can be downloaded from the web address mentioned below: http://ccl.northwestern.edu/netlogo/

This eBook contains the following chapters:

(i) The first chapter is an introduction of the eBook that provides readers the essential information regarding the field of Agent-based Computational Economics;

(ii) The second chapter describes the multi agent-based computational model of an artificial economy;

(iii) The third chapter describes the implementation in NetLogo of the multi agent-based model described in the second chapter;

(iv) The fourth chapter uses the computational model implemented in the third chapter for a set of computational experiments using NetLogo;

(v) The last chapter presents the results of the computational experiments conducted in the fourth chapter.

Alexandru Trifu

Faculty of Economics
"Petre Andrei" University of Iasi
Romania

PREFACE

Agent-based Computational Economics applies an interdisciplinary approach that combines knowledge from Agent-based Computational Modelling and Economics with the scope to observe, analyze and discuss the evolution of an economic system composed by intelligent agents. From 1990 till now, agent-based computational modelling has gained much attention but despite this phenomenon a fundamental issue is provoked by the next key question: Can agent-based computational model represent economic reality? To answer this, we must say that any agent-based model is a model of a real economic system that takes input data and creates output data by running computer experiments.

The development of theory and applications of agent-based computational models determined in the last years has brought a real revolution regarding the modelling of complex social systems. Presently, we can say that there is a real confrontation between the adepts of equation-based modelling and of agent-based modelling. A similar "war" was encountered at the end of 19th century and the beginning of 20th century between classical economic school and neoclassical one that lasted till the middle of 20th century with the victory of neoclassical school of Economics. Starting from 1990, Agent-based Economics started an offensive movement in order to obtain important position in the system of mainstream Economics.

The confrontation between these two modelling techniques can be won by agent-based modelling only if there lies a clear strategic plan that must be followed by the scientists that are adepts of this specific technique. In our opinion, this strategic plan must contain the following objectives:

(i)   Creating a general economic theory starting from the concept of agent considered as an entity that encapsulates parameters, variables, procedures and other sub-agents;

(ii)   Using this general theory, there must be created a set of agent-based models feasible for analyzing different aspects of economic reality;

(iii) This set of models must be implemented using a general software platform like for example NetLogo;

(iv) After implementing these models, then there must be created a set of computer games usable for training students in order to groom their abilities to be successful economic agents on real economic markets;

(v) We can draw the following features regarding the confrontation between adepts of equation-based and agent-based modelling in the field of Economics;

(vi) The adepts of agent-base modelling are fully offensive and this reality is proved by the increasing number of papers, books, software items that deal with the subject of Agent-based Computational Economics;

(vii) The adepts of equation-based modelling are in defensive positions and try to sustain their theories but the evolution of global economy encountered after 2008 is not in favour for such adepts;

(viii) The economic theory that utilizes agent-based modelling is still in the pipeline and it is hoped that such theory will become mature in the middle of 21st century;

(ix) If agent-based economic theory will gain the confrontation with equation-based theory then all the system of teaching economic sciences will dramatically change in the sense that students will use economic games implemented using agent-based modelling in order to obtain necessary abilities to be successful economic agents on real global economic market. At present, students memorize a set of economic theories that help them to pass exams; in the future, such students will have to pass "exams" implemented like economic games that will force our students to gain necessary abilities for becoming successful economic agents. This new training process will be exactly as the one used in our days for training pilots of airplanes; the pilot must pass the exam with flight simulator in order to become pilot of real airplanes. In other words, students must pass exams for administration of a simulated company implemented in the frame of an economic game in order to become active agent on real economic market.

Romulus-Catalin Damaceanu

Faculty of Economics,
"Petre Andrei" University of Iasi,
Romania
E-mail: romulus_catalin_damaceanu@yahoo.com

Send Orders of Reprints at bspsaif@emirates.net.ae
Agent-Based Computational Economics Using NetLogo, 2013, 3-18   **3**

CHAPTER 1

Introduction

Abstract: In this introductory chapter, we offer our readers the essential information regarding the field of Agent-based Computational Economics. The development of theory and applications of agent-based systems determined in the last years has brought a real revolution regarding the modelling of complex systems in the field of Economics. The main construction blocks of any agent-based computational model are the following: the set of agents (A), the initializations (I) and the simulation specifications (R). In order to validate an agent-based model, we must follow the following steps: (1) The analysis of pure theories of Economics; (2) Defining the objectives of research and the precise tasks of the model; (3) Building the conceptual model; (4) Validation of conceptual model; (5) Transformation of conceptual model in a computerized model using a software platform; (6) The operational validation of computerized model; (7) The analysis of experiments results and interpretation from an economic point of view.

Keywords: Agent-based Computational Economics, equation-based modelling, agent-based modelling, theory of systems, NetLogo software platform, conceptual and operational validation of agent-based models.

Agent-based Computational Economics applies an interdisciplinary approach that combines knowledge from Agent-based Computational Modelling and Economics with the scope to observe, analyze and discuss the evolution of an economic system composed by intelligent agents. Agent-based Computational Modelling involves research in areas of science where computing plays a central and essential role, emphasizing agents seen as entities that encapsulate other agents, procedures, parameters, and variables. Agent-based Computational Modelling is a branch of Applied Computational Mathematics that is currently the field of study concerned with constructing mathematical models and numerical solution techniques by using computers in order to analyze and solve scientific, social scientific and engineering problems (Damaceanu, 2010).

On the other hand, in Economics, the purpose of simulation tools was at the beginning purely theoretical and used equation-based modelling as we can see in (Fig. **1**) where from using the combination of definitions and assumptions, the scientist builds a theory (that in most cases is an equation-based model) to be confronted with the real economic phenomena. After the evaluation that uses

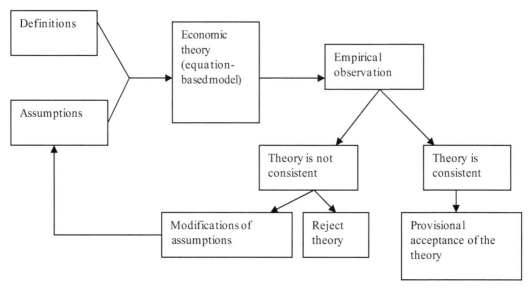

Figure 1: The process of creating an economic theory.

econometrics studies, the theory is considered consistent with the observed reality or non-consistent. In the first case, there is a provisional acceptance of the theory. In the second case, there is complete rejection or possibly changed assumptions as a result of observations made and the process is reconducted on new forms. This approach is motivated by the fact that since the middle of 20th century, equilibrium oriented approach was the mainstream developed to a highly sophisticated level by neoclassical economics. In the frame of mainstream economics, the theory is focused on static equilibrium (the dynamic equilibrium being approached as instant passing from one state of equilibrium to another as in Newton's Mechanics). The notion of equilibrium is used in many sciences as Mechanics, Thermodynamics, Biology, Economics, *etc.* to designate the state of a system that, in the absence of any external perturbation, can be maintained for an unlimited period. Thus, in Economics, the equilibrium can be defined according to this approach as the state when all economic agents are interested in not changing this state by using the available means of everyone. The standard general equilibrium model, conceived by Walras (1954) at the end of 19th century and formalized by Arrow *et al.* (1964), suggests that the continuity at the base of economic agents behaviour and technological changes, that combined with the convexity, generate the continual curves of offer and demand, and the existence of equilibrium. The associated linear models generated continual dynamics. For this type of models, it is very hard to obtain an algebraic formal solution. For example, even for the simplest model of world economy with two production factors and two products that uses Cobb-Douglass functions, the formal solution is very hard to find (Dinwiddy *et al.*, 1988). To find a numeric solution for this simplified model you must use computer programs. The development of numeric algorithms, that can be used to find the equilibrium solution for such simplified models, started 20-30 years ago (Shoven *et al.*, 1992).

The status of linearity of mainstream Economics can be changed by pressures coming from Mathematics and Physics. Inside Mathematics, two approaches were developed: one is axed on bifurcation and breaking of equilibrium in critical points, the other focuses on the idea that some functional relations considered linear are in fact nonlinear. These approaches are different in function of concentration on large-scale discontinuity (catastrophe theory), or small-scale discontinuity (chaos theory). The theory of catastrophe was developed in the first stage as a special case of bifurcation theory of Henry Poincare by Thom (1972) and Zeeman (1977). The bases of chaos theory were put by Lorenz (1963), Smale (1967), Mandelbrot (1982), and Mandelbrot (1989). Haken (1977, 1983) integrated these two theories by creating the synergetic theory in close relation with Prigogine (1980) theory of dissipative structures.

Economics are in natural continual evolution regarding as science. Regarding this aspect, West (1985) has distinguished five stages of scientific progress:

(i)   The verbal description of the subject and the logic of problem;

(ii) The formal identification of problem and quantification of mathematical relations;

(iii) Taking into account the dynamic aspects of mathematical model under the form of linear dynamic models;

(iv) The reconsideration of the basic scientific principles by including some nonlinear aspects in dynamic models;

(v)   The development of new complete nonlinear dynamic models able to explain all the possible phenomena described in the first stage.

For example, it is relatively easy to classify the economists in these five stages enumerated above. Thus, classical authors like Smith (1937), Ricardo (1951), and Malthus (1826) can be included in the first stage. The second stage is occupied by neoclassical economists like Marshall (1923), Walras (1954), and Pareto (1935). The sophisticated mathematical literature on the existence of equilibriums and their stability in the frame of general equilibrium scheme of such authors like Arrow (1964) can be assigned to the third stage. The literature of agent-based computational economics and evolutionary economics can be included in the fourth stage (Aruka, 2001; Boulding, 1991; Dosi *et al.*, 1994; Fagiolo *et al.*, 2004; Grebel *et al.*, 2003; Nelson *et al.*, 1982; Nelson, 1995; Page, 1997; Testfatsion, 2001a; Testfatsion, 2001b; Testfatsion, 2003; Vega-Redondo, 1996). An economic theory of nonlinear dynamics of fifth stage does not exist now. This eBook is intended to put the basis of such theory by speculating the development of theory and applications of Agent-based Computational Modelling in the field of Economics.

However, we must notice that despite increasing popularity, a fundamental issue is bring raised by the next key question: Can agent-based computational model represent economic reality? To answer this, we must say that any agent-based model is a model of a real economic system that takes input data and creates output data by running computer experiments - see (Fig. **2**).

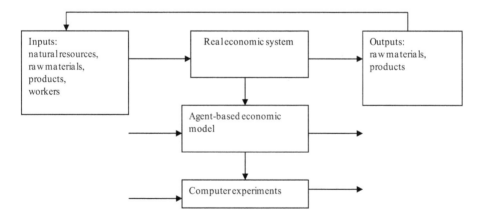

Figure 2: The relation between real economic system, economic theory/model and computer experiments.

(Fig. **2**) shows us that the real economic system uses inputs as natural resources (coal, oil, gas, minerals, water, plants, air, wind, sunlight, animals, forestry, pastures, soils *etc.*), raw materials, products, and workers to output raw materials and products that are re-entered as inputs in the next economic cycle of reproduction. In comparison with (Fig. **1**) we simply substitute equation-based models with agent-based models of economic systems, defined as follows: let P be some set of properties, R - a set of relationships, M - a set of objects. If on M there is a set of relations R, M is not necessarily a system. Objects M form a system only if the objects M carry out a set of relationships that we are interested for our scientific research. This means that the relations R must have fixed properties. Thus, we reach at the following definition: a set M of objects forms a system if it is carried on a given set of relationships R with fixed properties P. For example, if we look at an economic system, for the uninitiated, it will be presented as a simple set of economic entities, but for a specialist, it is a set with certain relationships having fixed properties. Systems can be categorized in different ways, particularly by the characteristics of properties P, of relations R and objects M.

The methodological principles for investigating systems are subject to general systems theory. The emergence of General systems theory is a natural consequence of specific cognitive difficulties in the study of complex objects in mathematics, physics, biology, economics, sociology, *etc.*, practically in all spheres of modern scientific knowledge. Today, for example, there are objects of science and practice living organisms, brains, economies *etc.* Difficulties of analysis and synthesis of such complex objects necessitated the creation of a special scientific instrument, usually known as systemic approach. The main categories of this approach are the concepts of system, structure, hierarchy, complexity *etc.*

The research of a system, which corresponds to different types of material and conceptual objects, is continuously raising a number of methodological problems that cannot be solved without recourse to some general processes of simplification and abstraction, and some new methods of modern mathematics. The general systems theory provides formal basis of methodological research of various kinds of objects viewed as systems. It does not replace the other sciences that examine such systems, but complements them.

The main features of the general theory of systems are reduced to the following:

(i)   It is based on the general scientific concept of system;

(ii) It includes all specialized systems theories: linear, nonlinear, axiomatic *etc.*;

(iii) The device used for research is the logic-mathematical apparatus;

(iv) It brings together theories on various aspects of system behaviour ;

(v)   It widespread by uses analogy and modelling methods.

The economic systems have dynamic behaviour. This means that as the flow of time passes, variables that measure their condition fluctuate significantly. We denote by *v(t)* the state of variable *v* at time t. To have a computer simulation of the dynamic behaviour of economic systems, it is necessary to obtain a model, a conventional image of the research object. The model is built by the subject of research to reflect the object characteristics (attributes, mutual relationships, structural and functional parameters, *etc.*) that are essential for research purposes. Therefore, the quality of this reflection, the extent to which the model is adequate to real economic system can properly be addressed only in relation to the established goal of research.

The model of economic system has practical significance because the analysis (through active experimentation with deductive research) with the means at the disposal of researcher is more accessible than the direct study of economic system. The premise of relatively higher accessibility to the analysis of the model compared with the economic system is given by the simplified picture (homomorphic) obtained by abstraction, neglecting the object properties that are not essential in terms of considered purpose.

Based on this simplified image, we can build the model of economic system isomorphic to the image formed previously on the set of attributes (or relations) established. More formalized one can say: two systems M_1 and M_2, each is the other model, if there is a homomorphic picture N_1 of system M_1 and homomorphic image N_2 of system M_2 that are isomorphic among themselves.

The model of economic system described in this eBook is abstract (conceptual) because characteristics P of objects M are described using a set of agents, and relations R are described by a set of procedures. The model is created by computer and is based on this conceptual model.

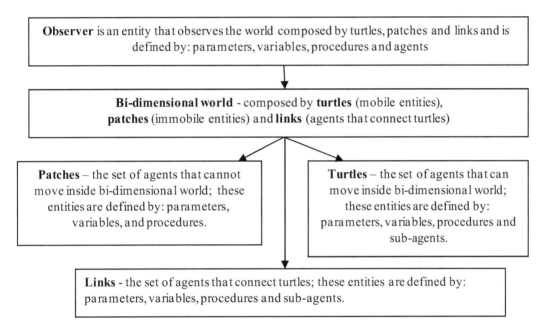

Observer is an entity that observes the world composed by turtles, patches and links and is defined by: parameters, variables, procedures and agents

Bi-dimensional world - composed by **turtles** (mobile entities), **patches** (immobile entities) and **links** (agents that connect turtles)

Patches – the set of agents that cannot move inside bi-dimensional world; these entities are defined by: parameters, variables, and procedures.

Turtles – the set of agents that can move inside bi-dimensional world; these entities are defined by: parameters, variables, procedures and sub-agents.

Links - the set of agents that connect turtles; these entities are defined by: parameters, variables, procedures and sub-agents.

Figure 3: The agents of NetLogo.

In the frame of this eBook, we try to see how we can use NetLogo software platform to create agent-based models of economic systems. NetLogo uses four types of agents: turtles, patches, links and observer – see (Fig. **3**). Turtles are agents that are moving inside the world. The world is a bi-dimensional lattice (an arrangement of objects in a regular periodic pattern) composed by patches. Links are agents that connect turtles. The observer does not have a specific location - we can imagine it like an entity that observes the world composed by turtles, patches and links. The active elements of the agent-based computational models are the set of procedures PRC because these are working with the other types of elements: parameters, variables and agents (the observer, turtles, links and patches). If the computational model did not have any procedure then it will not run. Under these circumstances, all the agent-based computational models implemented using NetLogo have at least one observer procedure. If this observer procedure does not exist than the computational models will not run because this declares all the parameters and initial variables, setup the patches, turtles and links, and calls the patches-own ($PRC(P_{xy})$), turtles-own ($PRC(T_i)$) and links-own procedures ($PRC(L_{ij})$) – see (Fig. **4**). With other words, the procedures are the active elements of agent-based models and the other elements (agents, parameters and variables) are the passive part. To understand better, we can make a comparison with an automobile that does not function if it does not have any fuel in the engine. Thus, the fuels of agent-based models are the procedures while agents, parameters, and variables compose the engine.

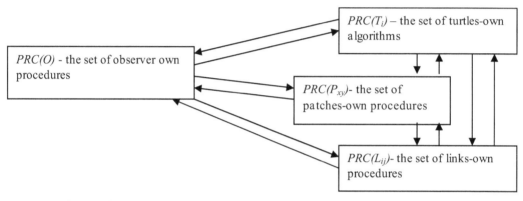

Figure 4: The set of procedures *PRC* - the active part of agent-based models.

The development of theory and applications of agent-based computational models determined in the last years has brought a real revolution regarding the modelling of complex social systems (Arthur *et al.*, 1997; Batten, 2000; Day *et al.*, 1993; Epstein *et al.*, 1996; Holland, 1992; Krugman, 1996; Sargent, 1993; Young, 1998; Gorobets *et al.*, 2006; Chen *et al.*, 2006; Dawid *et al.*, 2005; Marks, 2007; Gilbert, 2000). The history of the agent-based models can be traced back to the Von Neumann machine, a theoretical machine capable of reproduction (Neumann, 1966). The concept was improved by Stanislaw Ulam. Another improvement was brought by John Conway. He constructed the well-known Game of Life (Gardner, 1970). The birth of agent based modelling in social sciences was primarily brought by Craig Reynolds (Reynolds, 1987). Joshua M. Epstein and Robert Axtell developed the first large scale agent-based model, the Sugarscape, to simulate and explore the role of social phenomenon such as seasonal migrations, pollution, sexual reproduction, combat, and transmission of disease and even culture (Epstein *et al.*, 1996). More recently, Ron Sun developed methods for cognitive social simulation (Sun, 2006).

The main construction blocks of any agent-based computational model are the set of agents (A), the initializations (I), and simulation specifications (R) – see (Fig. **5**).

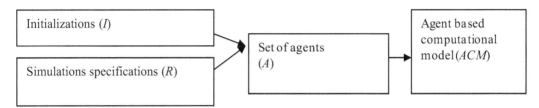

Figure 5: The elements of *ACM*.

The set of agents A contains all agents defined as artificial entities that encapsulate parameters, variables, procedures, and other sub-agents. Parameters have numerical values that do not modify on the entire period of simulation. Normally, parameters are initialized before simulation. However, in some situations they can be changed during the simulation. Variables are labels that exhibit a number of values during the simulation. Procedures are a finite list of well-defined operations that are working with the passive part of an-agent based computational (agents, parameters and variables) and with the active part (other procedures). In the frame of NetLogo there are two types of procedures: commands and reporters. A command is an action for an agent to carry out. A reporter computes a result and reports it. Other sub-agents are sub-entities of the agent.

Initializations I are a set of identities that have in left side the variable or parameter name and in the right side the associated value.

The simulation specifications R are a set of identities that have in the left side the control parameter name and in the right side the associated value.

Under these circumstances, an agent-based computational model (ACM) can be defined as a list of three arguments: the set of agents (A), the initializations (I) and simulation specifications (R). Shortly, *ACM = (A, I, R)*.

The study of *ACM* (Agent-based Computational Models) is concerned with the development and analysis of sophisticated artificial intelligence problem solvingIn for both single-agent and multiple-agent systems. These systems are also referred to as "self-organized systems" as they tend to find the best solution for their problems "without intervention".

In order to validate *ACM*, we must follow the following steps:

(i)   The analysis of real economic systems;

(ii)   Defining the objective of research and the precise task of the model;

(iii) Building the conceptual model;

(iv)   Validation of conceptual model;

(v)   Transformation of conceptual model in a computerized model using a software platform;

(vi)   The operational validation of computerized model;

(vii) The analysis of computer experiments results and interpretation from economic point of view. Based on these, we will formulate a number of conclusions.

To consider that *ACM* is conceptual validated, we have to accomplish a number of requirements. According to Heath (2010), these are the following:

(i)   Aids in learning and conveying system knowledge;

(ii)   Incorporates proper engineering judgment;

(iii) Aids in translating the conceptual model into a computerized model;

(iv)   Emphasizes the development and sanctioning of the micro-level behaviours;

(v)   Displays the theories and assumptions built into the model for quantitative analysis;

(vi)   Conveys the conceptual model 's logic and structure for qualitative analysis;

(vii) Completely represents the simulation so it can be reproduced by independent evaluators;

(viii) Provides justification for all structures and actions in the simulation;

(ix)   Reviewable by evaluators of varied simulation and domain expertise levels;

(x)   It can represent Disorganized and Organized Complex Systems;

(xi)   The operational validation of agent-based models has the following cycles - see (Fig. **6**):

 -   Cycle (1): modification of simulation specifications;

 -   Cycle (2): modification of parameters;

 -   Cycle (3): modification of initial values of variables;

 -   Cycle (4): modification of procedures;

 -   Cycle (5): development of new agents.

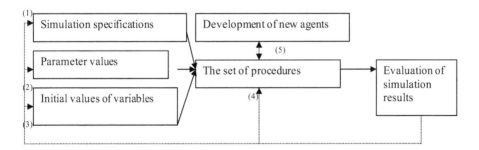

Figure 6: The cycles of operational validation of *ACM.*

Cycle (1) is used most frequently. In this case, the researcher uses a previous created *ACM* or a new one in an incipient form, modifies the simulation specifications, runs the model, evaluates the simulation results and in the light of these results takes the decision to apply one of the five available cycles.

Cycle (2) starts by changing the parameter values, running *ACM*, evaluation of results and in the light of outcomes the researcher applies one of the five cycles.

Cycle (3) modifies the initial values of variables, runs *ACM*, evaluates the results and considering these, the researcher takes the decision to apply one of the five cycles.

Cycle (4) modifies the set of procedures, runs the model and in the light of evolution results, the researcher applies one of the five cycles.

Cycle (5) develops new agents, runs the model and in the light of results, the researcher takes the decision to apply one of five available cycles. This cycle usually creates new *ACM*.

The operational validation of *ACM* is found to be different in the case of Economics if we compare with real sciences such as Physics, Biology, Chemistry, *etc.* On this issue, Cohen and Cyert state the next: "In social science, generally, the situation is [that] the behaviour of the total system can be observed. The problem is to derive a set of component relations, which will lead to a total system exhibiting the observed characteristics of behaviour. The procedure is to construct a model which specifies the behaviour of the components, and then analyze the model to determine whether or not the behaviour of the model corresponds with the observed behaviour of the total system" (Cohen *et al.*, 1961). Under these circumstances, the few quantitative measurements recorded are influenced by non-mechanic phenomena such as human behaviour and the reproduction of numerical series is very difficult. In other words, in the field of social sciences, the quantitative data are so insufficient and can be determined by a lot of processes that act in parallel that these data cannot be used to confirm or infirm a certain theory.

However, it is a well-known fact that many scientists use *ACM* in Economics. The purpose of this kind of research is to see what is going to happen if certain hypotheses are fulfilled, in other words to check whether a set of hypotheses are producing or not producing an expected set of results. In many cases, the expected results are not obtained and in this case, the researcher may find a new theory in order to find the cause of obtained data.

Those social sciences scientists that implement *ACM* for their research do not need to have a diploma in Computer Sciences. The necessary knowledge to write the source code for *ACM* implementation is minimal and is strongly connected with the functioning mechanism of *ACM* and less connected with knowing a certain programming language. If we take into consideration the Computer Sciences that are included in most of Economics curricula, then these skills are obtained during the training process of almost any Economics researcher.

Even if the necessary knowledge of *ACM* implementation is minimal, we must not forget that this job is still difficult and implies certain technical aspects that are sometimes not easy to deal with. Under these circumstances, we must follow a certain working methodology that is based on the next fundamental principles:

(i)   Implement just few code lines with minimal scientific meaning;

(ii) Add new lines only when the already added lines are extensively tested;

(iii) Start from the premise that any code line may contain an error.

The application of these principles is mandatory because the programming errors recognized by computer are only a small part of all possible errors. For example, the theoretical errors are very difficult to discover and correct. These are code lines that are correctly executed by computer but do not express the theoretical concepts of the researcher. To identify these errors, it is necessary not only to study in detail the code lines but also to analyze the entire set of obtained data produced by *ACM* implementation from the perspective of abstract theoretical concepts implemented by *ACM*.

CONFLICT OF INTEREST

The author(s) confirm that this article content has no conflict of interest.

ACKNOWLEDGEMENT

Declared none.

REFERENCES

Arrow, K.J., & Debreu, G. (1964). Existence of an Equlibrium for a Competitive Economy. *Econometrica, 22*, 265-290

Arthur, W.B., & Durlauf, S.N., Lane, D.A. (Eds.). (1997). *The economy as an evolving complex system II*. MA: Addison-Wesley

Aruka, Y. (2001). *Evolutionary Controversies in Economics : A New Transdisciplinary Approach*. Tokyo and Berlin: Springer

Batten, D. (2000). *Discovering artificial economics: How Agents Learn and Economies Evolve*. CO Boulder: Westview Press

Boulding, K.E. (1991). What is evolutionary economics?. *Journal of Evolutionary Economics, 1*, 9-17.

Chen, S.H., Tai, C.C. (2006). On the Selection of Adaptive Algorithms in ABM: A Computational-Equivalence Approach. *Computational Economics, 28*, 51-69

Cohen K., Cyert R. (1961). Computer models in dynamic economics. *Quarterly Journal of Economics, 75*(1), 112-127

Damaceanu, R. C. (2010). *Applied Computational Mathematics in Social Sciences*. Sharjah: Bentham Science Publishers

Dawid, H., & Reimann, M. (2005). Evaluating Market Attractiveness: Individual Incentives *Versus* Industry Profitability. *Computational Economics, 24*, 321-355

Day, D., & Chen, P. (1993). *Nonlinear Dynamics and Evolutionary Economics*. Oxford, UK: Oxford University Press

Dinwiddy, C. L., & Teal, F. J. (1988). *The two-sector General Equlibrium Model: A new Approach*. Oxford: Philip Allan

Dosi, G. & Orsenigo, L., (1994). Macrodynamics and microfoundations: an evolutionary perspective. In: Granstrand, O. (ed.). *The economics of technology*. Amsterdam: North Holland

Epstein, J.M., & Axtell, R. (1996). *Growing Artificial Societies: Social Science from the Bottom Up*. Cambridge, MA: MIT Press

Fagiolo, G., & Dosi, G., Gabriele, R. (2004). Matching, Bargaining, and Wage Setting in an Evolutionary Model of Labor Market and Output Dynamics. *Advances in Complex Systems, 14*, 237-273.

Gardner, M. (1970). Mathematical Games - The fantastic combinations of John Conway's new solitaire game "life". *Scientific American, 223*, 120-123

Gilbert, N., & Terna, P. (2000). How to build and use agent-based models in social science. *Mind & Society, 1*, 57-72

Gorobets, A., Nooteboom, B. (2006). Adaptive Build-up and Breakdown of Trust: An Agent Based Computational Approach. *Journal of Management and Governance, 10*, 277-306

Grebel, T., & Pyka, A., Hanusch, H. (2003). An Evolutionary Approach to the Theory of the Entrepreneur. *Industry and Innovation, 10*, 493-514.

Haken, H. (1983). *Advanced Synergetics*. Berlin, Heidelberg: Springer

Haken, H. (1977). *Synergetics: An Introduction*. Berlin, Heidelberg: Springer

Heath, L. B. (2010). *A Diagram for Conceptual Validation of Agent-based Models, A dissertation submitted in partial fulfillment of the requirements for the degree of Doctor of Philosophy*. Wright State University, http://etd.ohiolink.edu/send-pdf.cgi/Heath%20Brian%20L.pdf?wright1269176275;

Holland, J. (1992). Adaptation in Natural and Artificial Systems. Cambridge, MA: The MIT Press

Krugman, P. (1996). *The self-organizing economy*. Cambridge, MA: Blackwell Publishers

Lorenz, E. (1963). Deterministic Nonperiodic Flow. *J. Atmos. Sci.*, *20*, 130-141

Malthus, Th. R. (1826). *An Essay on the Principle of Population*. London: John Murray

Mandelbrot, B.B. (1989). *Les objets fractals*. Paris: Flammarion

Mandelbrot, B.B. (1982). *The Fractal Geometry of Nature*. New York: W. H. Freeman and Co.

Marks, R.E. (2007). Validating Simulation Models: A General Framework and Four Applied Examples. *Computational Economics*, *30*, 265-290

Marshall, A. (1923). *Money, Credit, and Commerce*. London: MacMillan and Co., Ltd.

Nelson, R.R., & Winter, S.G. (1982). *An Evolutionary Theory of Economic Change*. Cambridge, MA: Cambridge University Press

Nelson, R.R. (1995). Recent Evolutionary Theorizing About Economic Change. *Journal of Economic Literature*, *33*, 48-90

Neumann, J. (1966). *Theory of Self-Reproducing Automata*. Urbana and London: University of Illinois Press

Page, S.E. (1997). On Incentives and Updating in Agent Based Models. *Computational Economics*, *10*, 67-87

Pareto, V. (1935). *The Mind and Society [Trattato Di Sociologia Generale]*. Harcourt: Brace

Prigogine, I. (1980). *From being into Becoming: Time and Complexity in Physical Sciences*. San Francisco: Freeman

Reynolds, C. (1987). Flocks, herds and schools: A distributed behaviour al model. *Proceedings of the 14th annual conference on Computer graphics and interactive techniques*, 25-34

Ricardo, D. (1817). *Principles of Political Economy and Taxation*. Reprinted in: Sraffa, P. (Ed.), (1951). *The works and Correspondance of David Ricardo*. London: Cambridge University Press

Sargent, T. (1993). *Bounded Rationality in Macroeconomics*. Oxford, UK: The Arne Ryde Memorial Lectures, Clarendon Press

Shoven, J.B., & Whalley, J. (1992). *Applying General Equlibrium*. Cambridge: Cambridge University Press

Smale, S., (1967). Differential Dynamical Systems, *Bulletin of the American Mathematical Society*, *73*, 747-817

Smith, A. (1937). *An inquiry into the nature and causes of the wealth of nations*. New York: Cannan Edition, American Modern Library Series

Sun, R. (2006). *Cognition and Multi-Agent Interaction: From Cognitive Modeling to Social Simulation*. Cambridge: Cambridge University Press

Tesfatsion, L. (2002). Agent-based Computational Economics : Growing Economies from the Bottom Up. *Working Paper, No.1*, Iowa State University, Dept. of Economics

Tesfatsion, L. (2001a). Agent-based modelling of evolutionary economic systems. *IEEE Transactions on Evolutionary Computation*, *5*, 1-6

Tesfatsion, L. (2001b). Structure, Behaviour , and Market Power in an Evolutionary Labor Market with Adaptive Search. *Journal of Economic Dynamics and Control*, *25*, 419-457

Thom, R. (1972). *Stabilite structurelle et Morphogenese*. New York: Benjamin

Vega-Redondo, F. (1996). *Evolution, Games, and Economic Behaviour* . Oxford: Oxford University Press

Walras, L. (1954). *Elements of Pure Economics*. Homewood: Irwin

West, B.J. (1985). *An Essay on the Importance of Being Nonlinear*. Berlin-Heidelberg-New York: Springer

Young, H.P. (1998). *Individual Strategy and Social Structure*. Princeton, NJ: Princeton University Press

Zeeman, E.C. (1977). *Catastrophe Theory: Selected Papers (1972-1977)*. Mass.: Addison-Wesley Reading

Send Orders of Reprints at bspsaif@emirates.net.ae

CHAPTER 2

The Multi Agent-Based Computational Model of an Artificial Economy

Abstract: In this chapter, we describe the multi agent-based computational model of an artificial economy and proceed to the conceptual validation process by describing the observer O with its parameters, variables, procedures and sub-agents T_i and P_{xy}.

Keywords: Validation of conceptual model, parameters, variables, procedures, agents, sub-agents.

The multi agent-based computational model of an artificial economy created using NetLogo has the following characteristics:

(i)   The mobile agents called turtles T_i are of two types: consumers CO_i and producers PR_i;

(ii) Consumers are in number of $m = \{1,2,3,..,100\}$ and producers are in number of $n = \{1,2,3,..,100\}$;

(iii) The immobile agents P_{xy} have a certain amount of resources $0 \leq r_{xy} \leq 10$, where x, y are integer numbers in interval $[-20,20]$;

(iv) Consumers obtain their income by extracting resources and selling them to producers for a certain price rs_{it} that is the amount of money offered for every unit of harvested resources.

(v)   Producers buy resources from consumers and process these resources to produce goods;

(vi) Consumers buy goods from producers; usually, every consumer has a need of one unit of the good produced by producers per every period if the available income permits him to buy this unit;

(vii) Every consumer uses two matching algorithms: one is used for selling resources to producers; the other is used for buying products;

(viii) Every producer has the liberty, on one hand, to set the price pr_{it} of his product in order to obtain more incomes by selling products to consumers, and, on the other hand, to set the price rs_{it} of the resources purchased from consumers.

THE VALIDATION OF CONCEPTUAL MODEL

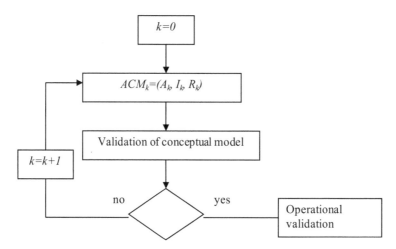

Figure 1: The process of building the conceptual model.

An agent-based computational model (*ACM*) is a list of three arguments: the set of agents (*A*), the initializations (*I*) and the simulation specifications (*R*) (Damaceanu, 2010). The process of building the conceptual model can be defined like constructing the initial set of agents (A_0), setting the initial values of initializations (I_0) and specifying the initial values for simulation specifications (R_0) - see (Fig. **1**), for a graphical description of the process. This figure shows us how the initial form of the ACM_0 enters in the phase of conceptual validation. If this validation fails the conceptual model is modified in a new form ACM_1 and the process is reiterated until conceptual validation is a success and the model become subject to operational validation.

The validation of conceptual model is a process that checks the integrity of all component elements of agent based model ACM_k divided in three major sets: the set of agents A_k, the set of initializations I_k and the set of simulation specifications R_k. In our case, because the model is developed in the frame of NetLogo software platform, we have the following set $A_k = \{O, T_i, P_{xy}\}$, where O is the observer agent that does not have a specific location - we can imagine it like an entity that observes the world composed by its sub-agents turtles T_i, and patches P_{xy} - see (Fig. **2-6**) (Wilensky, 1999).

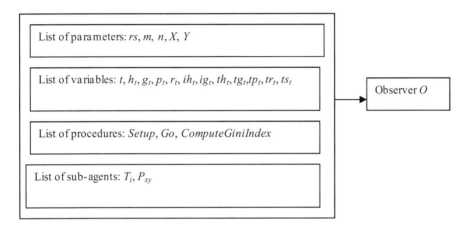

List of parameters: rs, m, n, X, Y

List of variables: $t, h_t, g_t, p_t, r_t, ih_t, ig_t, th_t, tg_t, tp_t, tr_t, ts_t$

List of procedures: *Setup, Go, ComputeGiniIndex*

List of sub-agents: T_i, P_{xy}

Observer O

Figure 2: The elements of observer O.

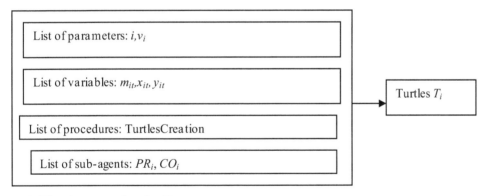

List of parameters: i, v_i

List of variables: m_{it}, x_{it}, y_{it}

List of procedures: TurtlesCreation

List of sub-agents: PR_i, CO_i

Turtles T_i

Figure 3: The elements of turtles T_i.

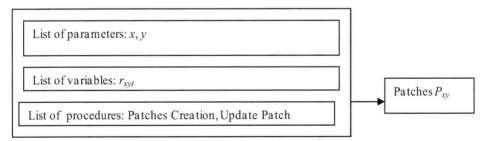

List of parameters: x, y

List of variables: r_{xyt}

List of procedures: Patches Creation, Update Patch

Patches P_{xy}

Figure 4: The elements of patches P_{xy}.

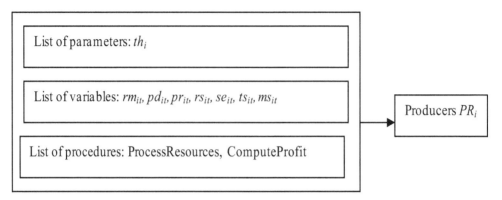

Figure 5: The elements of producers PR_i.

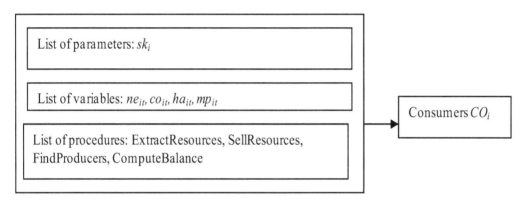

Figure 6: The elements of consumers CO_i.

The second set is $I_k = (IO, IT_i, IP_{xy})$, where IO are the initializations of O, where IT_i are the initializations of T_i and IP_{xy} are the initializations of P_{xy} - see Tables **1-5**, and the third set is $R_i = (rs, m, n)$, where:

- $rs = \{0, -1, 1, -2, 2\}$ is the seed of pseudorandom generator used by NetLogo. The seed may be any integer in the range supported by NetLogo (-9007199254740992 to 9007199254740992). In the context of scientific modeling, pseudo-random numbers are actually desirable. That is because it is very important for a scientific experiment to be reproducible;

- $m = \{1,2,3,.., 100\}$ is the number of consumers;

- $n = \{1, 2, 3,.., 100\}$ is the number of producers.

Table 1: Initializations of O

Item	Description
$rs = \{0, -1, 1, -2, 2\}$	A parameter used to set the seed of the pseudo-random number generator.
$m = \{1,2,3,..,100\}$	A parameter used to set the number of consumers
$n = \{1,2,3,..,100\}$	A parameter used to set the number of producers
$t = 0$	This variable keeps the time of simulation
$h_t = 0$	This variable keeps the mean value of Herfindahl index (also known as Herfindahl–Hirschman Index, or HHI) that measures the amount of competition among producers using formula: $h_t = \dfrac{th_t}{t}$
$g_t = 0$	This keeps the mean value of Gini coefficient that measures the inequality among population of consumers regarding the amount of money. It is computed using formula: $g_t = \dfrac{tg_t}{t}$
$p_t = 0$	Keeps the mean value of prices for products: $p_t = \dfrac{tp_t}{t}$
$r_t = 0$	Keeps the mean value of prices for resources: $r_t = \dfrac{tr_t}{t}$
$ts_t = 0$	Keeps total value of output for products: $ts_t = \displaystyle\sum_{i=1}^{n} ts_{it}$
$ih_t = 0$	This index is computed using formula: $ih_t = \displaystyle\sum_{i=1}^{n} ms_{it}^2$, where ms_{it}^2 is the market share of producer $i = \overline{1,n}$
$ig_t = 0$	This coefficient is computed using formula: $ig_t = \dfrac{A_t}{A_t + B_t}$ where A_t is the area between the line of perfect equality and the Lorenz curve, and B_t is the area under the Lorenz curve.
$th_t = 0$	This variable is computed using formula $th_t = th_{t-1} + ih_t$
$tg_t = 0$	This variable is computed using formula $tg_t = tg_{t-1} + ig_t$
$tp_t = 0$	This variable is computed using formula $tp_t = tp_{t-1} + p_t$
$tr_t = 0$	This variable is computed using formula $tr_t = tr_{t-1} + r_t$

Table 2: Initializations of T_i

Item	Description
i = a value from the set $\{1,2,.., m+n\}$	The identification number of the turtle
v_i = a random value from the set $\{1, 2,.., 10\}$	A parameter that describes the vision of turtle (how many patches ahead a turtle can see)
m_{it} = a random value from the set $\{500,501,..,999\}$	The amount of money
x_{it} = a value from the set $\{-X, -X+1,.., 0, 1,.., X\}$	Identify the horizontal coordinate of turtle, where $X = 20$ is the maximum x coordinate.
y_{it} = a value from the set $\{-Y, -Y+1,.., 0, 1,.., Y\}$	Identify the vertical coordinate of turtle, where $Y = 20$ is the maximum y coordinate.

Table 3: Initializations of P_{xy}

Item	Description
x = a value from the set $\{-X, -X+1,.., 0, 1,.., X\}$	Parameters that identify the horizontal coordinate of patch, where $X = 20$ is the maximum x coordinate for patch
y = a value from the set $\{-Y, -Y+1,.., 0, 1,.., Y\}$	Parameters that identify the vertical coordinate of patch, where $Y = 20$ is the maximum y coordinate for patch
r_{xyt} = a random value from the set $\{0, 1, 2,.., 9\}$	A variable owned by patch that keeps the value of resources

Table 4: Initializations of PR_i

Item	Description
th_i = a random value from the interval $[0.1,1]$	This parameter describes the technological capability of producer
$rm_{it} = 0$	Keeps the amount of raw material
pd_{it} = a random value from the set $\{500,501,502,..,999\}$	Keeps the amount of products
pr_{it} = a random value from the set $\{1,23\}$	Keeps the value of price for products
$rs_{it} = 1$	Keeps the value of price for resources
se_{it} = a random value from the set $\{1,23\}$	Keeps the amount of products sold in period t
$ts_{it} = 0$	Keeps the total amount of products sold: $ts_{it} = ts_{it-1}+se_{it}$
$ms_{it} = 0$	Keeps the value of market share: $ms_{it} = ts_{it} / ts_t$

Table 5: Initializations of CO_i

Item	Description
sk_i = a random value from the interval [0.1,1]	This parameter describes the skill to extract resources of consumer
ne_{it} = {0,1}	This variable has two possible values: 0 when the need for products is not satisfied and 1 otherwise
co_{it} = a random value from the set {500,501,502,..,999}	Keeps the value of products available for consumption
ha_{it} = 0	Keeps the amount of harvested resources
$mp_{it} = \Phi$	Keeps the identification number of producer where the consumer is going to buy products

THE DESCRIPTION OF OBSERVER O

The observer O is the root agent of any agent-based computational model that is going to be implemented in the frame of NetLogo software platform. This artificial entity embeds the following elements:

(i) Parameters:

- rs is a parameter used to set the seed of the pseudo-random number generator;

- m is used to set the number of consumers;

- n is used to set the number of producers.

(ii) Variables:

- t is a variable that keeps the time of simulation;

- h_t is a variable that keeps the mean value of Herfindahl index (also known as Herfindahl–Hirschman Index, or HHI) that measures the amount of competition among producers using formula: $h_t = \dfrac{th_t}{t}$;

- g_t is a variable that keeps the mean value of Gini coefficient that measures the inequality among population of turtles regarding the amount of money. It is computed using formula: $g_t = \dfrac{tg_t}{t}$;

- p_t is a variable that keeps the mean value of prices for products: $p_t = \dfrac{tp_t}{t}$;

- s_t is a variable that keeps the mean value of output for products: $s_t = \dfrac{ts_t}{t}$;

- ih_t is a index is computed using formula: $ih_t = \sum\limits_{i=1}^{n} ms_{it}^2$, where ms_{it}^2 is the market share of producer $i = \overline{1,n}$;

- ig_t is a coefficient computed using formula: $ig_t = \dfrac{A_t}{A_t + B_t}$ where A_t is the area between the line of perfect equality and the Lorenz curve, and B_t is the area under the Lorenz curve;

- th_t is a variable computed using formula $th_t = th_{t-1} + ih_t$;

- tg_t is a variable computed using formula $tg_t = tg_{t-1} + ig_t$;

- tp_t is a variable computed using formula $tp_t = tp_{t-1} + p_t$;

- tr_t is a variable computed using formula $tr_t = tr_{t-1} + r_t$;

- ts_t is a variable computed using formula $ts_t = ts_{t-1} + s_t$.

(iii)   Procedures:

- *Setup* is the procedure used to make the necessary initializations in order to start the simulation and it is initiated when we press the button <Setup> on NetLogo interface:

Step 1. Clear all agents used in previous simulations

Step 2. Set the value of random number generator to *rs*

Step 3. Call procedure *PatchesCreation*

Step 4. Call procedure *TurtlesCreation*

Step 5. Call procedure *SetupPlots*

Step 6. Call procedure *UpdatePlots*

- *Go* is the procedure used to run simulation and it is initiated when we press the button <Go> on NetLogo interface:

Step 1. Set t: = t+1

Step 2. Ask consumers CO_i to set Ne_{it}: = 0

Step 3. Ask producers PR_i to set se_{it}: = 0 and call procedure *Process Resources*

Step 4. Ask consumers CO_i to call procedure *ExtractResources*, *Update Patch*, *SellResources*

Step 5. Ask consumers CO_i with $ne_{it} = 0$ to call procedure *Find Producers*, *ComputeBalance*

Step 6. Ask producers PRi to:

- call procedure *ComputeProfit*

- if $\sum_{i=1}^{n} ts_{it} > 0$ then set ms_{it}: $= \dfrac{ts_{it}}{\sum_{i=1}^{n} ts_{it}}$

Step 7. Set h_t: $= \sum_{i=}^{n} ms_{it}^{2}$

Step 8. Set th_t: $= th_t + h_t$

Step 9. Set h_t: $= th_t / t$

Step 10. Set tg_t: $= tg_t + g_t$

Step 11. Set g_t: $= tg_t / t$

Step 12. Set $tp_t := tp_t + \dfrac{\sum\limits_{i=1}^{n} pr_{it}}{n}$

Step 13. Set $p_t := tp_t / t$

Step 14. Set $r_t := tr_t + \dfrac{\sum\limits_{i=1}^{n} rs_{it}}{n}$

Step 15. Set $r_t := tr_t / t$

Step 16. Set $ts_t := \sum\limits_{i=}^{n} se_{it}$

Step 17. If $t = 1000$ the stop simulation

- *ComputeGiniIndex* is the procedure used to compute Gini index:

Step 1. Create the following local variables SW_t, TW_t, WS_t, GI_t, IR_t and set $SW_t :=$ a sorted list of consumers in function of consumer own variable m_{it}, $TW_t := \sum\limits_{i=1}^{m} m_{it}$, $WS_t := 0$, $GI_t := 0$, $IR_t := 0$

Step 2. Repeat m times the following sequence for $i = \{1,2,..,m\}$:

- Set $WS_t := WS_t + m_{it}$
- Set $GI_t := GI_t + 1$
- Set $IR_t := IR_t + (GI_t/m) - (WS_t/TW_t)$

Step 3. Set $ig_t := (IR_t/m)/0.5$

  (iv)   Sub-agents: T_i, P_{xy}.

THE DESCRIPTION OF TURTLES T_i

The turtles T_i are the mobile agents used by NetLogo software platform. This type of artificial entity embeds the following elements:

(i) Parameters:

- i - is the identification number of the turtle;

- v_i - is a parameter that describes the vision of turtle (how many patches ahead a turtle can see).

(ii) Variables:

mo_{it} - the amount of money;

x_{it} - the horizontal coordinate;

y_{it} - the vertical coordinate.

(iii) Procedures:

- *TurtlesCreation* is the procedure used to set up the turtles:

Step 1. Create n producers PR_i with the settings:

i: = a value from the set $\{1,2,..,n\}$

x_{it}: = a random value from the set $\{-20,-19,-18,..,0,1,2,.20\}$

y_{it}: = a random value from the set $\{-20,-19,-18,..,0,1,2,.20\}$

v_i: = a random value from the set $\{1,2,3,..,10\}$

mo_{it}: = a random value from the set $\{500,501,502,..,999\}$

$th_{i:}$ = a random value from the interval $[0.1,1]$

rm_{it}: = 0

$pd_{it:}$ = a random value from the set $\{500,501,502,..,999\}$

pr_{it}: = a random value from the set $\{1,23\}$

$rs_{it}: = 1$

$se_{it}: =$ a random value from the set $\{1,23\}$

$ms_{it}: = 0$

Step 2. Create m consumers CO_i with the settings:

$i: =$ a value from the set $\{n+1,n+2,.,n+m\}$

$x_{it}: =$ a random value from the set $\{-20,-19,-18,.,0,1,2,.20\}$

$y_{it}: =$ a random value from the set $\{-20,-19,-18,.,0,1,2,.20\}$

$v_i: =$ a random value from the set $\{1,2,3,.,10\}$

$mo_{it}: =$ a random value from the set $\{500,501,502,.,999\}$

$sk_{i:} =$ a random value from the interval $[0.1,1]$

$ne_{it}: = \{0,1\}$

$co_{it} =$ a random value from the set $\{500,501,502,.,999\}$

$ha_{it} = 0$

$mp_{it} = \Phi$

(iv) Sub-agents PR_i, CO_i: First type of sub-agents, PR_i are the producers that buy resources from consumers CO_i and try to sell the products obtained after processing these resources.

PR_i embeds the following elements:

(i) Parameters:

-    i - is the identification number of the producer from the set $\{1,2,.,n\}$.

(ii) Variables:

$th_{i:}$ - a parameter that describes technical ability of producer to obtain products from raw materials and has a value from the interval [0.1,1];

rm_{it} - the amount of raw materials

pd_{it} - the amount of production

pr_{it} - the price of product

rs_{it} - the price of resources (raw materials)

se_{it} - the amount of production sold

ts_{it} - the total amount of products sold

ms_{it} - the value of market share

(iii) Procedures:

ProcessResources, ComputeProfit. The first procedure *ProcessResources* is described below:

Step 1. Set $pd_{it}: = pd_{it-1} + th_i \cdot rm_{it}$

Step 2. Set $rm_{it}: = 0$

ComputeProfit is described below:

Step 1. Set $ts_{it}: = ts_{it-1} + se_{it}$

Step 2. If n>1 then execute:

if $ts_{it}/ts_t \leq 1/n$ then execute:

if $pr_{it} > 1.01$ then execute:

set $pr_{it}: = pr_{it} - 0.01$

if $rs_{it} < pr_{it}$ then execute:

set $rs_{it}: = rs_{it} + 0.01$

otherwise execute:

$rs_{it} := pr_{it} - 0.01$

otherwise execute:

set $pr_{it} := pr_{it} + 0.01$

if $rs_{it} > 1.01$ then execute:

$rs_{it} := rs_{it} - 0.01$

Step 3. If $se_{it} > 1$ then execute:

set $pr_{it} := pr_{it} + 0.01$

Step 4. If $se_{it} = 0$ then execute:

select a random patch in radius of vision v_i

CO_i embeds the following elements:

(i) Parameters:

-   i - the identification number of the consumer from the set $\{n+1, n+2, .., n+m\}$.

(ii) Variables:

x_{it} - the horizontal coordinate from the set $\{-20, -19, -18, .., 0, 1, 2, .20\}$

y_{it} - the vertical coordinate from the set $\{-20, -19, -18, .., 0, 1, 2, .20\}$

sk_i - describes the skill to extract resources of consumer and has value from the interval $[0.1, 1]$

ne_{it} - has two possible values: 0 when the need for products is not satisfied and 1 otherwise;

co_{it} - the value of products available for consumption;

ha_{it} - the amount of harvested resources;

mp_{it} - the identification number of producer where the consumer is going to buy products.

(iii)   Procedures:

ExtractResources, SellResources, FindProducers, ComputeBalance.

First procedure ExtractResources is detailed below:

Step 1. If $r_{xyt} = 0$ then execute:

let lo_{xy} be the coordinates of a patch with maximum value of r_{xyt} in radius of vision vi

if $lo_{xy} \neq \Phi$ and $lo_{xy} \neq P_{xy}$ then execute:

set heading towards location lo_{xy}

move forward towards location lo_{xy}

Step 2. If $r_{xyt} \geq sk_i$ then execute:

set $ha_{it}: = ha_{it} + sk_{it}$

set $r_{xyt}: = r_{xyt} - sk_{it}$

otherwise execute:

set $ha_{it}: = ha_{it} + r_{xyt}$

set $r_{xyt}: = 0$

Second procedure SellResources is described below:

Step 1. Let be mc_i my own identification number

Step 2. Let mp_i the identification number of one producers in radius v_i with maximum value for rs_{it}

If $mc_i \neq \Phi$ then execute:

move to producer mp_i

ask producer mp_i to execute:

let q_i: $= ha_i$ of consumer mc_i

if $mo_{it} \geq = q_i \cdot rs_{it}$ then execute:

set rm_{it}: $= rm_{it} + ha_{it}$ of consumer mc_i

set ha_{it} of consumer mc_i: $= 0$

set mo_{it} of consumer mc_i: $= (mo_{it}$ of consumer $mc_i) + q_i \cdot rs_{it}$

set mo_{it}: $= mo_{it} - q_i \cdot rs_{it}$

otherwise execute:

set heading to a random direction

move forward with vision v_i patches

Third procedure *FindProducers* is presented here:

Step 1. If $ne_{it} = 0$ then execute:

let be mc_i my own identification number

let mp_i the identification number of one producers in radius v_i with minimum value for pr_{it}

if $mp_i \neq \Phi$ then execute:

move to producer mp_i

ask producer mp_i to execute:

if $pd_{it}>1$ and $(mo_{it}$ of $mc_i) \geq pr_{it}$ then execute:

set $(co_{it}$ of $mc_i) := (co_{it}$ of $mc_i)+1$

set (moit of mci) := $(mo_{it}$ of $mc_i)-pr_{it}$

set $se_{it} := se_{it}+1$

set $pd_{it} := pd_{it}-1$

set $mo_{it} := mo_{it}+pr_{it}$

otherwise execute

set heading to a random direction

move forward with vision v_i patches

Fourth procedure *ComputeBalance* has the following content:

Step 1. If $ne_{it} = 0$ and $co_{it} \geq = 1$ then execute:

set $co_{it} := co_{it}-1$

set $ne_{it} := 1$

THE DESCRIPTION OF PATCHES P_{xy}

The patches P_{xy} are the immobile agents used by NetLogo software platform. This type of artificial entity embeds the following elements:

(i) Parameters:

-    x - identify the horizontal coordinate of patch.

-    y - identify the vertical coordinate of patch.

(ii) Variable r_{xyt} keeps the value of resources.

(iii) Procedures:

- Procedure *PatchesCreation* is used for setting up the patches:

Step 1. Ask all patches P_{xy} to set r_{xyt}: = a random value from the set $\{0,1,2,..,9\}$

Step 2. Color patch P_{xy} in yellow in function of variable r_{xyt}

- Procedure *UpdatePatch* is described below:

Step 1. Color patch P_{xy} in yellow in function of variable r_{xyt}

CONFLICT OF INTEREST

The author(s) confirm that this article content has no conflict of interest.

ACKNOWLEDGEMENT

Declared none.

REFERENCES

Damaceanu, R. C. (2011). *Agent-based Computational Social Sciences using NetLogo*. Germany: Lambert Academic Publishing.

Damaceanu, R. C. (2010). *Applied Computational Mathematics in Social Sciences*. Sharjah: Bentham Science Publishers.

Wilensky, U. (1999). *NetLogo*. http://ccl.northwestern.edu/netlogo/. Center for Connected Learning and Computer-Based Modeling. Evanston, IL: Northwestern University.

Send Orders of Reprints at bspsaif@emirates.net.ae

Agent-Based Computational Economics Using NetLogo, 2013, 37-71   37

CHAPTER 3

The Implementation in NetLogo of the Multi Agent-Based Model

Abstract: The implementation of the conceptual model using NetLogo is the process of transforming the algorithms described in Chapter 2 in procedures recognized by NetLogo. Any agent-based computational model implementation must be operational validated and verified. A model is considered operational valid to the extent provides a satisfactory range of if it accuracy consistent with the intended application of the model.

Keywords: Implementation of conceptual model, evolutionary system, NetLogo software platform, observer, turtles and patches own procedures.

Agent-based modeling facilitates a more direct correspondence between the entities in the target system and the parts of the model that represent them and enhances the descriptive accuracy of the modeling process, but it can also create difficulties (Edmonds, 2001). Under these circumstances, almost every implementation of agent-based models may contain bugs defined as code that does something different in comparison with what you expected (Gilbert, 2007). As Axelrod (1997) underlines, you have to work hard to confirm that the implemented model was correctly programmed. Axtell and Epstein state that "the robustness" of macrostructures to perturbations in individual agent performances is specific to agent-based models and makes very hard to identify bugs (Axtell *et al.*, 1994).

An-agent based model implementation is the result of three different types of scientist: the thematician, the modeller and the computer scientist (Drogoul *et al.*, 2003). Thus, discovering inconsistencies in programming languages lines is in general a difficult task. Several authors have identified the concept of ontology (Christley *et al.* 2004; Pignotti *et al.*, 2005; Polhill *et al.*, 2006; Polhill 2007), defined as formal, explicit specification of a shared conceptualization (Gruber, 1993), to be particularly promising for this purpose, especially in the domain of agent-based social simulation.

The implementation of the conceptual model using NetLogo is the process of transforming the algorithms described in Chapter 2 in procedures recognized by NetLogo. Any agent-based computational model implementation must be operational validated and verified. A model is operational valid to the extent that it provides a satisfactory range of accuracy consistent with the intended application of the model (Kleijnen, 1995; Sargent, 2003). Thus, if the objective is to accurately represent social reality, then validation is about assessing how well the model is capturing the essence of its empirical referent. This could be measured in terms of goodness of fit to the characteristics of the model's referent (Moss *et al.*, 1997). Verification (sometimes called "internal validation" (Taylor, 1983; Sansores *et al.*, 2005; Stanislaw, 1986; Richiardi *et al.* 2006) is the process of ensuring that the model performs in the manner intended by its designers and implementers. Thus, verification is the process of looking for errors. An example of an implementation error would be the situation where the programmer intends to loop through the whole list of agents in the program, but he mistakenly writes the code so it only runs through a subset of them. A less trivial example of an error would be the situation where it is believed that a program is running according to the rules of real arithmetic, while the program is actually using floating-point arithmetic (Polihill *et al.*, 2005; Polhill *et al.*, 2005b; Polhill *et al.*, 2006; Izquierdo *et al.*, 2006).

GENERAL CHARACTERISTICS OF NETLOGO SOFTWARE PLATFORM

NetLogo is a software platform designed by Uri Wilensky it in the year 1999 (Wilensky, 1999). NetLogo is in a process of development and modernization in the frame of Center for Connected Learning and Computer-Based Modeling - Northwestern University, Illinois, USA. NetLogo is written in Java language and can be run on all major platforms (Windows, Mac, Linux *etc.*). In addition, individual models can be run as Java applets inside web pages. NetLogo is freeware and can be downloaded from the next web address: http://ccl.northwestern.edu/netlogo/. For the moment there are available the next versions of NetLogo: NetLogo4.1beta1, NetLogo4.0.4, NetLogo3DPreview5, NetLogo 3.1.5, NetLogo 3.0.2, NetLogo2.1, NetLogo2.0.2, and NetLogo1.3.1 – see (Fig. **1**). From this list, I selected NetLogo 4.0.5 and I used this version for implementing the model described in Chapter 2 of this eBook.

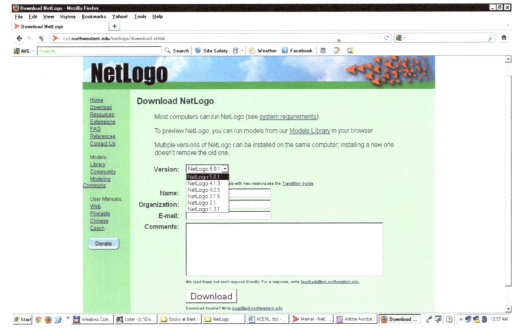

Figure 1: The available versions of NetLogo.

NetLogo is used for modeling complex systems developing over time. You can give instructions to hundreds or thousands of agents operating concurrently. This makes it possible to explore the connection between the micro-level behaviour of individuals and the macro-level patterns that result from the interactions of agents.

NetLogo has a Models Library with a large collection of agent-based models that can be used and/or modified. These address many areas in the natural and social sciences, including biology and medicine, physics and chemistry, mathematics and computer science, economics and social psychology. Netlogo uses three types of agents: turtles, patches and observer. When NetLogo is run first time, there are no turtles. The observer can create new turtles. In addition, the patches can do the same thing. Turtles and patches have coordinates determined by the variables xcor and ycor for turtles and, respectively, pxcor and pycor for patches. The patch with the coordinate (0,0) is called origin. pxcor is growing (pxcor>0) if we are moving to the right and is dropping (pxcor<0) if we are moving to the left in comparison with the origin. In the same time, pycor is growing (pycor>0) if we are moving up and is dropping (pycor<0) if we are moving down in comparison with the origin.

The total number of patches is determined by the parameters min-pxcor, max-pxcor, min-pycor, and max-pycor.

In NetLogo, the procedures are of two types: commands and reporters. A command is an action that an agent must execute. A reporter calculates a result and reports it. NetLogo uses four types of variables: global variables, turtles variables, patches variables and system variables. The first type of variables may be accessed by any type of agent. The next two types can be accessed only by the agent inside whom the variables were created. The last type of variables is predefined by NetLogo. Examples of system variable are the next: color (sets the color of turtle), pcolor (sets the color of patch), xcor, ycor, heading (sets the orientation in space of turtles), pxcor (the horizontal coordinate of a patch), pycor (the vertical coordinate of a patch) *etc.*

In NetLogo, you have the choice of viewing models found in the Models Library, adding other models to existing ones, or creating your own models. The NetLogo interface was designed to meet all these needs. The interface is divided into two main parts: NetLogo menus and the main NetLogo window. The main window is divided into the next tabs: "Interface", "Procedures" and "Information". Only one tab at a time can be visible, but you can switch between them by clicking on the tabs at the top of the window. Right below the row of tabs is a toolbar containing a row of buttons. The available buttons vary from tab to tab. The "Interface" tab is where you watch the running of model. This tab also has tools that you can use to inspect and alter what is going on inside the model. When you first open NetLogo, the "Interface" tab is empty except for the View, where the turtles and patches appear, and the Command Center, which allows you to enter NetLogo commands.

The "Procedures" tab is the workspace where the code for the model is stored. The commands that you only want to use immediately go in the Command Center; the commands that you want to save and use later, over and over again, are found in the "Procedures" tab.

The "Information" tab provides an introduction to the model and an explanation of how to use it, things to explore, possible extensions, and NetLogo features.

NetLogo has the next defining characteristics:

(i)   Simplicity: NetLogo models are created without major technical difficulties and, under these conditions, the scientist can concentrate only on modeling problems. NetLogo offer a software platform that can be used even by no experienced programmers;

(ii)   Transparency: NetLogo models contain only the elements that are explicitly included by modeller. Every element can be documented is accessible using NetLogo interface;

(iii)   Gradual modeling: NetLogo permit a gradual development of models and by using this method you can avoid the traps of complexity;

(iv)   Cross-platform: runs on Mac, Windows, Linux, *etc.*;

(v)   Extensive options of running: any model can be run in many ways;

(vi)   Environment: you can view your model in either 2D and 3D;

(vii)   Behaviour Space tool used to collect data from multiple runs of a model;

(viii) System Dynamics Modeller;

(ix)   Speed slider lets you fast forward your model or see it in slow motion;

(x)   Powerful and flexible plotting system;

(xi)   HubNet: participatory simulations using networked devices;

(xii)   Models can be saved as applets to be embedded in web pages.

A program written in NetLogo consists of optional declarations (globals, breed, turtles -own, patches -own, <BREED>-own) in any order, followed by zero or more procedure definitions. Every procedure definition begins with to or to-report, the procedure name, and an optional bracketed list of input names. Every procedure definition ends with end. In between are zero or more commands.

Commands take zero or more inputs; the inputs are reporters, which may also take zero or more inputs. No punctuation separates or terminates commands; no punctuation separates inputs. Identifiers must be separated by whitespace or by parentheses or square brackets. (So for example, a+b is a single identifier, but a(b[c]d)e contains five identifiers).

All commands are prefix. All user-defined reporters are prefix. Most primitive reporters are prefix, but some (arithmetic operators, Boolean operators, and some agent-set operators like with and in-points) are infix.

All commands and reporters, both primitive and user-defined, take a fixed number of inputs by default. Some primitives are variadic, that is, may optionally take a different number of inputs than the default; parentheses are used to indicate this, *e.g.* (list 1 2 3) (since the list primitive only takes two inputs by default). Parentheses are also used to override the default operator precedence, *e.g.* (1 + 2) * 3, as in other programming languages.

Sometimes an input to a primitive is a command block (zero or more commands inside square brackets) or a reporter block (a single reporter expression inside square brackets). User-defined procedures may not take a command or reporter block as input.

Operator precedences are as follows, high to low:

(i)   with, at-points, in-radius, in-cone

(ii)   (all other primitives and user-defined procedures)

(iii)   ^

(iv)   *,/, mod

(v)   +, -

(vi)   <, >, <=, >=

(vii)   =, !=

(viii) and, or, xor

A GENERAL DESCRIPTION OF THE MODEL IMPLEMENTED IN NETLOGO

The agent-based model described in this chapter is seen as an economic system that function in a bi-dimensional space composed by 1681 patches P_{xy} - see (Fig. 2). As (Fig. 1) shows us, the bi-dimensional space is a square with a side of 41 patches. In reality, (Fig. 1) does not show us the true image of the bi-dimensional space because in our case the so called square is in reality a torus defined as a toroid generated by a circle, a surface having the shape of a doughnut. - see (Fig. 3). The dimension of this space is in function of two parameters: $X=20$ which is the maximum horizontal coordinate for patch and $Y=20$ which is the maximum vertical coordinate for patch - see (Fig. 4). In this bi-dimensional space, there is a mobile agent called turtle T_i that has the ability to move on patches P_{xy}. In fact, there are two types of mobile agents: one is called PR_i and the other is called consumer CO_i - - see Fig. 5.

Figure 2: The bi-dimensional space composed by patches $P_{xy.}$

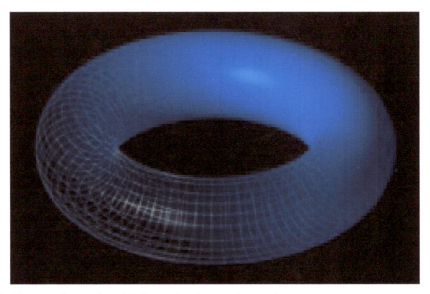

Figure 3: The true shape of the bi-dimensional space (a torus).

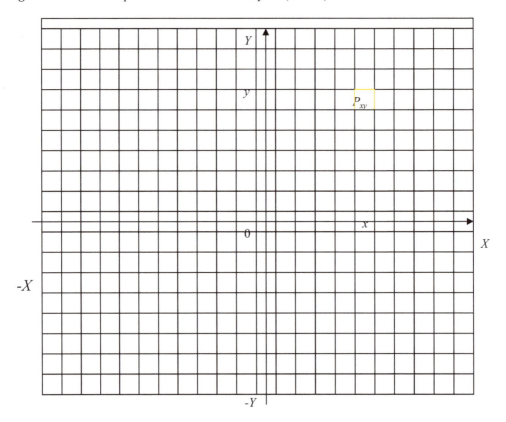

Figure 4: The dimension of space is controlled by parameters X and Y.

The shape of producer PR_i

The shape of consumer CO_i

Figure 5: The shapes of producer PR_i and of consumer CO_i.

The general description of this model implemented in NetLogo is presented in (Fig. **6**) and in Tables **1-5** we have the description of agents (observer, turtles, patches, producers, and consumers) seen from NetLogo perspective.

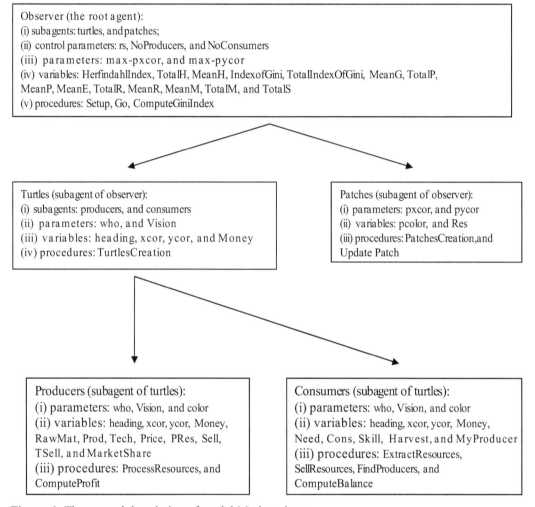

Figure 6: The general description of model Market.nlogo

Table 1: Parameters, variables and procedures used by observer

Label	Label used by NetLogo	Type	Description
rs	rs	control parameter (simulation specification)	A parameter used to set the seed of the pseudo-random number generator

Table 1: contd....

m	NoConsumers	control parameter (simulation specification)	A parameter used to set the number of consumers
n	NoProducers	control parameter (simulation specification)	A parameter used to set the number of producers
t	ticks	variable	This variable keeps the time of simulation
h_t	MeanH	variable	This variable keeps the mean value of Herfindahl index (also known as Herfindahl–Hirschman Index, or HHI) that measures the amount of competition among producers using formula: $h_t = \dfrac{th_t}{t}$
g_t	MeanG	variable	Keeps the mean value of Gini coefficient that measures the inequality among population of consumers regarding the amount of money. It is computed using formula: $g_t = \dfrac{tg_t}{t}$
p_t	MeanP	variable	Keeps the mean value of prices for products: $p_t = \dfrac{tp_t}{t}$
r_t	MeanR	variable	Keeps the mean value of prices for resources: $r_t = \dfrac{tr_t}{t}$
ts_t	TotalS	variable	Keeps total value of output for products: $ts_t = \displaystyle\sum_{i=1}^{n} ts_{it}$

Table 1: contd….

ih_t	HerfindahlIndex	variable	This index is computed using formula: $ih_t = \sum_{i=1}^{n} ms_{it}^2$, where ms_{it}^2 is the market share of producer $i = \overline{1,n}$
ig_t	IndexofGini	variable	This coefficient is computed using formula: $ig_t = \dfrac{A_t}{A_t + B_t}$ where A_t is the area between the line of perfect equality and the Lorenz curve, and B_t is the area under the Lorenz curve.
th_t	TotalH	variable	This variable is computed using formula $th_t = th_{t-1} + ih_t$
tg_t	TotalIndexOfGini	variable	This variable is computed using formula $tg_t = tg_{t-1} + ig_t$
tp_t	TotalP	variable	This variable is computed using formula $tp_t = tp_{t-1} + p_t$
tr_t	TotalR	variable	This variable is computed using formula $tr_t = tr_{t-1} + r_t$
Setup	Setup	procedure	This is the procedure used to make the necessary initializations in order to start the simulation and it is initiated when we press the button <Setup> on NetLogo interface.
Go	Go	procedure	This is the procedure used to run simulation and it is initiated when we press the button <Go> on NetLogo interface.
ComputeGiniIndex	ComputeGiniIndex	procedure	This is the procedure used to compute Gini index.

Table 1: contd….

| T_i | turtles | sub-agent | These are the mobile agents used by NetLogo software platform. |
| P_{xy} | patches | sub-agent | These are the immobile agents used by NetLogo software platform. |

Table 2: Parameters, variables and procedures used by turtles

Label	Label used by NetLogo	Type	Description
i	who	parameter	It holds the turtle's "who number" or ID number, an integer greater than or equal to zero.
v_i	vision	parameter	A parameter that describes the vision of turtle (how many patches ahead a turtle can see).
m_{it}	money	variable	The amount of money
x_{it}	xcor	variable	Identify the horizontal coordinate of turtle
y_{it}	ycor	variable	Identify the vertical coordinate of turtle
TurtlesCreation	TurtlesCreation	procedure	The procedure used to set up the turtles
PR_i	producers	sub-agent	the producers
CO_i	consumers	sub-agent	the consumers

Table 3: Parameters, variables and procedures used by patches

Label	Label used by NetLogo	Type	Description
x	pxcor	parameter	This keeps the horizontal coordinate of patch.
y	pycor	parameter	This keeps the vertical coordinate of patch.
r_{xyt}	Res	variable	This keeps the value of resources.

Table 3: contd....

| PatchesCreation | PatchesCreation | procedure | This is used for setting up the patches. |
| UpdatePatch | UpdatePatch | procedure | This is used for updating patches. |

Table 4: Parameters, variables and procedures used by producers

Label	Label used by NetLogo	Type	Description
th_i	Tech	parameter	This parameter describes the technological capability of producer.
rm_{it}	RawMat	variable	Keeps the amount of raw material
pd_{it}	Prod	variable	Keeps the amount of products
pr_{it}	Price	variable	Keeps the value of price for products
rs_{it}	PRes	variable	Keeps the value of price for resources
se_{it}	Sell	variable	Keeps the amount of products sold in the current period
ts_{it}	TSell	variable	Keeps the total amount of products sold
ms_{it}	MarketShare	variable	Keeps the value of market share
ProcessResources	ProcessResources	procedure	The procedure used for processing resources to obtain products.
ComputeProfit	ComputeProfit	procedure	The procedure used to compute profit.

Table 5: Parameters, variables and procedures used by consumer

Label	Label used by NetLogo	Type	Description
sk_i	Skill	parameter	This parameter describes the skill to extract resources of consumer
ne_{it}	Need	variable	This variable has two possible values: false when the need for products is not satisfied and true otherwise

Table 5: contd….

co_{it}	Cons	variable	Keeps the value of products available for consumption
ha_{it}	Harvest	variable	Keeps the amount of harvested resources
mp_{it}	MyProducer	variable	Keeps the identification number of producer where the consumer is going to buy products
ExtractResources	ExtractResources	procedure	The procedure used for extracting resources
SellResources	SellResources	procedure	The procedure used for selling resources to producers
FindProducers	FindProducers	procedure	The procedure used to find the producer where to buy products
ComputeBalance	ComputeBalance	procedure	The procedure used to compute the balance of incomes and expenses

The model Market.nlogo implemented in NetLogo contains three tabs. First tab is the Interface tab is where you watch the model run – see (Fig. **7**), the second is Information tab provides an introduction to the model and an explanation of how to use it, things to explore, possible extensions, and NetLogo features – see (Fig. **8**), and the last is Procedures tab that is the workspace where the code for the model is stored – see (Fig. **9**).

Figure 7: The interface tab.

Figure 8: The information tab.

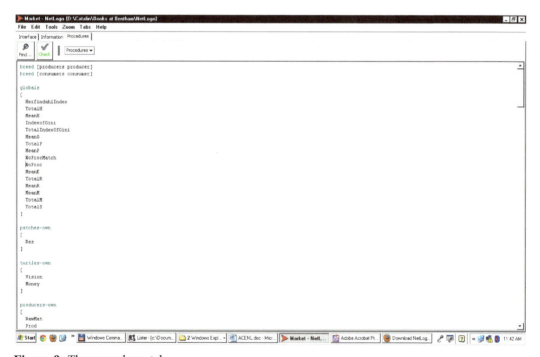

Figure 9: The procedures tab.

IMPLEMENTATION OF OBSERVER AGENT

The observer -own procedures are the code lines written in NetLogo located in the next sections:

(i)　globals[.];

(ii)　patches-own[.];

(iii)　turtles-own[.];

(iv)　producers-own;

(v)　consumers-own;

(vi)　to Setup. end;

(vii)　to Go. end;

(viii) to ComputeGiniIndex. end.

The keyword globals[.] can only be used at the beginning of a program, before any function definitions. It defines new global variables or parameters. Global variables are accessible by all agents and can be used anywhere in a model. Most often, globals[.] is used to define variables or constants that need to be used in many parts of the program. In the following paragraphs, there are described the code lines assigned to observer agent. In our case, we defined the next new global variables and parameters: HerfindahlIndex (this variable keeps the value of Herfindahl index (also known as Herfindahl–Hirschman Index, or HHI) that measures the amount of competition among producers), TotalH (the total value of Herfindahl–Hirschman Index), MeanH (the average value of Herfindahl–Hirschman Index), IndexofGini (keeps the value of Gini coefficient that measures the inequality among population of consumers regarding the amount of money), TotalIndexOfGini (the total value of Gini coefficient), MeanG (the average value of Gini coefficient), TotalP (the total value of prices for products), MeanP (the average value of prices for products), TotalR (the total value of prices for resources), MeanR (the average value of prices for resources), TotalS (the total value of output for products) – see the next code lines:

```
globals
[
HerfindahlIndex
TotalH
MeanH
IndexofGini
TotalIndexOfGini
MeanG
TotalP
MeanP
TotalR
MeanR
TotalS
]
```

The keyword patches-own can only be used at the beginning of a program, before any function definitions. It defines the variables and parameters that all patches can use. All patches will then have the given variables and be able to use them. All patch variables can also be directly accessed by any turtle standing on the patch. In our model, we defined the variable Res that keeps the value of resources: – see the next code lines:

```
patches -own
[
Res
]
```

The turtles-own keyword can only be used at the beginning of a program, before any function definitions. It defines the variables and parameters belonging to each turtle. Our model uses the next: Vision (a parameter that describes the vision of turtle - how many patches ahead a turtle can see), and Money (the amount of money) – see the next code lines.

```
turtles -own
[
Vision
Money
]
```

The producers-own keyword can only be used at the beginning of a program, before any function definitions. It defines the variables and parameters belonging to each producer: RawMat (keeps the amount of raw material), Prod (keeps the amount of products), Tech (this parameter describes the technological capability of producer), Price (keeps the value of price for products), PRes (keeps the value of price for resources), Sell (keeps the amount of products sold in one period), TSell (keeps the total amount of products sold), and MarketShare (keeps the value of market share) – see the next code lines.

```
producers-own
[
RawMat
Prod
Tech
Price
PRes
Sell
TSell
MarketShare
]
```

The consumers-own keyword can only be used at the beginning of a program, before any function definitions. It defines the variables and parameters belonging to each producer: Need (this variable has two possible values: 0 when the need for products is not satisfied and 1 otherwise), Cons (keeps the value of products available for consumption), Skill (this parameter describes the skill to extract resources of consumer), Harvest (keeps the amount of harvested resources), MyProducer (keeps the identification number of producer where the consumer is going to buy products) – see the next code lines.

```
consumers-own
[
Need
Cons
Skill
Harvest
MyProducer
]
```

The procedure Setup makes the necessary steps in order to initiate the computer simulation – see the code lines below. The keyword to is used to begin a command procedure. The first command is ca that resets all global variables to zero, and calls reset-ticks (resets the tick counter to zero), clear-turtles (kills all turtles and resets the who numbering, so the next turtle created will be turtle 0), clear-patches (clears the patches by resetting all patch variables to their default initial values, including setting their color to black), clear-drawing (clears all lines and stamps drawn by turtles), clear-all-plots (clears every plot in the model), and clear-output (Clears all text from the model's output area).

The next line uses the command random-seed that sets the seed of the pseudo-random number generator. The seed may be any integer in the range supported by NetLogo (-9007199254740992 to 9007199254740992). The random numbers used by NetLogo are what is called "pseudo-random". That means they appear random, but are in fact generated by a deterministic process. "Deterministic" means that you get the same results every time, if you start with the same random "seed".

The next three lines call the procedures PatchesCreation (creates three types of patches: food, energy and water), TurtlesCreation (creates the initial number of turtles), UpdateSocialClass (used to update the social classes), and ComputeGiniIndex (used to compute Gini index).

The final line of procedure Setup is the keyword end used to conclude a procedure.

```
to Setup
ca
random-seed rs
PatchesCreation
TurtlesCreation
ComputeGiniIndex
end
```

The procedure Go starts the computer simulation. The first command is tick that advances the tick counter by one. The next line uses the command ask that runs the given commands for the specified agent or agentset. In our case all consumers run the next command block [set Need false] that set the value of variable need to false which means that all consumers have the need to consume one unit of product for the respective period of time.

The next line asks to all producers to set the value of sell variable to 0 and runs the procedure ProcessResources used from processing resources to obtain products.

The following line asks all consumers to run the procedures ExtractResources (used for extracting resources from patches), UpdatePatch (used to update the colour of patches), and SellResources (used for selling resources to producers).

The following line asks all consumers with the value of variable need set to false to run procedures FindProducers (used for finding a producers that have products for sell), and ComputeBalance (used for computation of financial balance).

The following line asks all producers to run procedure ComputeProfit (used for computing the profit) and to calculate the value of marketshare.

The following two lines check if the number of producers and/or consumers is equal with zero and if this is true the simulation is stopped. The reporter used is count that reports the number of agents in the given agentset.

The following twelve lines compute the value of the following variables: HerfindahlIndex (this variable keeps the value of Herfindahl index, also known as Herfindahl–Hirschman Index, or HHI, that measures the amount of competition among producers), TotalH (total value of Herfindahl–Hirschman Index), MeanH (mean value of Herfindahl–Hirschman Index), TotalIndexOfGini (keeps the mean value of Gini coefficient that measures the inequality among population of consumers regarding the amount of money), MeanG (mean value of Gini coefficient), TotalP (keeps the total value of prices for products), MeanP (keeps the mean value of prices for products), TotalR (keeps the total value of prices for resources), MeanR (keeps the mean value of prices for resources), and TotalS (keeps total value of output for products).

The following line runs the procedure ComputeGiniIndex used to compute Gini index.

The last line stops the simulation if ticks reports 1000. The procedure ticks reports the current value of the tick counter. The result is always a number and never negative. Most models use tick command to advance the tick counter, in which case ticks will always report an integer. If the tick-advance command is used, then ticks may report a floating point number.

```
to Go
tick
ask consumers [set Need false]
ask producers [set Sell 0 ProcessResources]
ask consumers
```

[ExtractResources

UpdatePatch

SellResources]

ask consumers with [Need = False] [FindProducers ComputeBalance]

ask producers

[ComputeProfit ComputeGiniIndex

if sum [TSell] of producers > 0 [set MarketShare TSell/sum [TSell] of producers]]

if count producers = 0 [stop]

if count consumers = 0 [stop]

set HerfindahlIndex sum [MarketShare * MarketShare] of producers

set TotalH TotalH + HerfindahlIndex

set MeanH TotalH/ticks

set TotalIndexOfGini TotalIndexOfGini + IndexOfGini

set MeanG TotalIndexOfGini/ticks

set TotalP TotalP + mean [Price] of producers

set MeanP TotalP/ticks

set TotalR TotalR + mean [PRes] of producers

set MeanR TotalR/ticks

set TotalM TotalM + mean [Money] of consumers

set MeanM TotalM/ticks

set TotalS sum [TSell] of producers

if ticks = 1000 [stop]

end

The procedure ComputeGiniIndex is used to compute Gini index. The first line of this procedure is used to create a temporary sorted list containing the list of variables money owned by consumers in ascending order. The second line create a temporary variable TotalWealth that keeps the total sum of money of consumers. Next lines create temporary variables WealthSumSoFar, GiniIndex, and GiniIndexReserve.

The following line uses repeat that runs a block of commands for how many consumers are times. The block of commands which is repeated set the values of WealthSumSoFar, GiniIndex, and GiniIndexReserve in order to compute the value of IndexOfGini in the last line of this procedure.

```
to ComputeGiniIndex

let SortedWealths sort [Money] of consumers

let TotalWealth sum SortedWealths

let WealthSumSoFar 0

let GiniIndex 0

let GiniIndexReserve 0

repeat count consumers [

set    WealthSumSoFar    (WealthSumSoFar    +    item    GiniIndex
SortedWealths)

set GiniIndex (GiniIndex + 1)

set GiniIndexReserve GiniIndexReserve + (GiniIndex/count consumers)
- (WealthSumSoFar/TotalWealth)]

set IndexOfGini (GiniIndexReserve/count consumers)/0.5

end
```

IMPLEMENTATION OF TURTLES AGENTS

Procedure TurtlesCreation is the only procedure assigned to turtles and uses the commands create-producers NoProducers [commands] and create-consumers NoConsumers [commands] that creates NoProducers new producers and NoConsumers new consumers. If commands are supplied, the new turtles immediately run commands - see the code lines listed below;

to TurtlesCreation

create-producers NoProducers

[setxy random-xcor random-ycor

set color red

set vision 1 + random 10

set Prod 500 + random 500

set Money 500 + random 500

set Price 1 + random 3

sct PRes 1

set Tech 0.1 + random-float 1 if Tech > 1 [set Tech 1]

set Sell 1 + random 3

set TSell TSell + Sell

if TSell > 0 [set MarketShare TSell/sum [TSell] of producers]]

create-consumers NoConsumers

[setxy random-xcor random-ycor

set color green

set vision 1 + random 10

set Money 500 + random 500

set Need false

set Cons 500 + random 500

set Skill 0.1 + random-float 1 if Skill > 1 [set Skill 1]

set MyProducer nobody]

end

The block of commands in the case of producers contains the following:

-   Command setxy x y that sets its horizontal coordinate to x and vertical
    coordinate to y. Equivalent to set xcor x set ycor y, except it happens

in one time step instead of two. If x or y is outside the world, NetLogo will throw a runtime error but in our case this is prevented by using the reporters random-xcor and random-ycor that report a random floating point number from the allowable range of turtle coordinates along the given axis, x or y;

-   The colour of producer is set to red by using the built-in variable color that can be represented either as a NetLogo colour (a single number), or an RGB colour (a list of 3 numbers). If you use a single number then this one must be in the range 0 to 139.9. (Fig. **10**) is showing the range of colours you can use in NetLogo. The second colour representation in NetLogo is an RGB (red/green/blue) list. When using RGB colours the full range of colours is available to you. RGB lists are made up of three integers between 0 and 255. The Color Swatches dialog helps us to experiment with and choose favourite colours. It can be opened by choosing Color Swatches on the Tools Menu - see (Fig. **11**);

-   The following lines set the values of parameters and variables: vision, Prod, Money, Price, PRes, Tech, Sell, TSell, and MarketShare. Some of these settings are operated using the reporters random and random-float. random number reports a random integer greater than or equal to 0, but strictly less than number if number is positive. If number is negative, it reports a random integer less than or equal to 0, but strictly greater than number. If number is zero, the result is always 0 as well. random-float number reports a random floating point number greater than or equal to 0 but strictly less than number if number is positive. If number is negative, it reports a random floating point number less than or equal to 0, but strictly greater than number. If number is zero, the result is always 0.

The block of commands in the case of consumers contains the following:

-   Setting the coordinates and colour of producers in a similar manner as in the case of consumers;

-   Setting the values of parameters and variables: vision, Money, Need, Cons, Skill, and MyProducer. For variable MyProducer, there is used nobody which is a special value for some primitives such as turtle, one-of, max-one-of, *etc.* This indicates that no agent was found. Also, when a turtle dies, it becomes equal to nobody.

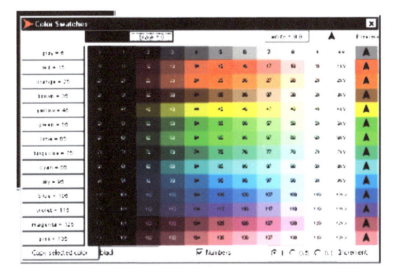

Figure 10: The colours of NetLogo.

Figure 11: The colour swatches dialog.

IMPLEMENTATION OF PATCHES AGENTS

The paches -own procedures are the code lines written in NetLogo located in the sections:

(i) to PatchesCreation. end;

(ii) to UpdatePatch. end.

The first procedure PatchesCreation is used to set the values of variables Res (the amount of resources available on every patch) and pcolor (the colour of the patch). To set the colour of patches, we used the reporter scale-color color number range1 range2. This reports a shade of color proportional to number. If range1 is less than range2, then the larger the number, the lighter the shade of color. But if range2 is less than range1, the color scaling is inverted. If number is less than range1, then the darkest shade of color is chosen. If number is greater than range2, then the lightest shade of color is chosen.

```
to PatchesCreation
ask patches
[set Res Random 10
set pcolor scale-color yellow Res 0 9]
end
```

The second procedure is used to update the colour of a patch using the same reporter scale-color.

```
to UpdatePatch
set pcolor scale-color yellow Res 0 9
end
```

IMPLEMENTATION OF PRODUCERS AGENTS

The producers -own procedures are the code lines written in NetLogo located in the sections:

(i) to ProcessResources. end;

(ii) to ComputeProfit. end.

The first procedure ProcessResources is used to simulate the transformation process of resources (raw materials) in finite products. For this to the previous value of production amount Prod is added a new quantity obtained by multiplying the value of technological coefficient Tech with the value of raw materials (resources) RawMat obtained from consumers in the current period of time. At the end the value of RawMat is set to zero which means that all the quantity was used for producing goods.

```
to ProcessResources
set Prod Prod + Tech * RawMat
set RawMat 0
end
```

The second procedure ComputeProfit is used by every producer to compute the profit at the end of every time period. The first line of this procedure set the value of variable TSell used to keep the value of total sells.

The next line is used by every producer to evaluate his position on the market and in function of situation he can take the following decisions:

- In the case when his market share is less or equal with $\frac{1}{n}$ then if Price > 1.01 then the price is decremented with 0.01; if PRes < Price then the price of resources is incremented with 0.01, otherwise the price of resources is set tot the value Price - 0.01;

- In the case when his market share is higher than $\frac{1}{n}$ then if Price > 1.01 then the price is incremented with 0.01; if PRes < Price then the price of resources is decremented with 0.01, otherwise the price of resources is set tot the value Price - 0.01;

- If Sell > 1 then the price is incremented with 0.01;

- If if Sell = 0 then the producer take the decision to relocate his business. To simulate such decision we used the reporter one-of patches that reports a random patch. If the agentset is empty, reports nobody. If this situation is encountered then the producer simply sets a random heading and goes forward vision patches.

to ComputeProfit

set TSell TSell + Sell

ifelse count producers > 1

[if sum [Tsell] of producers != 0

[ifelse TSell/sum [TSell] of producers <= 1/count producers

[if Price > 1.01 [set Price Price - 0.01 ifelse PRes < Price [set PRes PRes + 0.01] [set PRes Price - 0.01]]]

[set Price Price + 0.01 if PRes > 1.01 [set PRes PRes - 0.01]]]]

[if Sell > 1

[set Price Price + 0.01]]

if Sell = 0

[let random-move one-of patches in-radius vision

ifelse random-move != nobody [move-to random-move] [set heading random 360 fd vision]]

if Money < 0 [die]

end

IMPLEMENTATION OF CONSUMERS AGENTS

The consumers -own procedures are the code lines written in NetLogo located in the sections:

(i) to ExtractResources. end;

(ii) to SellResources. end;

(iii) to FindProducers. end;

(iv) to ComputeBalance. end.

The first procedure ExtractResources is used by every consumer to extract resources Res from patches. The first line of this procedure checks if Res = 0 and if this is true then the consumer looks for a patch with maximum value for resources Res in the radius of his vision. To find this patch in his vision we used the reporter max-one-of agentset [reporter] that reports the agent in the agentset that has the highest value for the given reporter. If max-one-of reports other value than nobody and the patch where the consumer is sitting then the heading is set towards to the respective patch and the consumer moves to that patch using the reporter distance agent that reports the distance from this agent to the calling turtle or patch.

The next line checks if Res >= Skill and if this is true then value of variable Harvest (the amount of harvested resources) is incremented with the value of Skill, and the value of variable Res is decremented with the value of Skill. Otherwise, the value of Harvest is incremented with the value of Res, and the value of Res is set to 0.

```
to ExtractResources
if Res = 0
[let location max-one-of patches in-radius vision [Res]
if location != nobody and location != patch-here
[set heading towards location
fd distance location]]
ifelse Res >= Skill [set Harvest Harvest + Skill set Res Res - Skill] [set
Harvest Harvest + Res set Res 0]
end
```

The second procedure SellResources is used by every consumer to sell his harvested resources to a certain producer found in the radius of his vision. First line of this procedure creates a temporary variable MyConsumer using command let variable value that creates a new local variable and gives it the given value. A local variable is one that exists only within the enclosing block of commands. In the same line is used self that reports this consumer.

The next line set the value of consumer-own variable MyProducer using the reporter max-one-of producers in-radius vision [PRes] that return the producer that has the maximum price of resources PRes in the radius of vision of consumer.

The next line checks if the variable MyProducer is different than nobody and if this is true then is executed a command block that simulate the process of selling resources to the selected producer, otherwise the consumer set his heading to a random value and moves forward vision patches.

```
to SellResources
let MyConsumer self
set MyProducer max-one-of producers in-radius vision [PRes]
ifelse MyProducer != nobody
[move-to MyProducer
ask MyProducer
[let q [Harvest] of MyConsumer
if Money >= q * PRes
[set RawMat RawMat + [Harvest] of MyConsumer
set [Harvest] of MyConsumer 0
set [Money] of MyConsumer [Money] of MyConsumer + q * PRes
set Money Money - q * PRes]]]
[set heading random 360 fd vision]
end
```

The third procedure FindProducers is used by every consumer to find a certain producer suitable for buying his products available for sell.

```
to FindProducers

if Need = false

[let MyConsumer self

set MyProducer min-one-of producers in-radius vision [Price]

ifelse MyProducer != nobody

[move-to MyProducer

ask MyProducer

[if Prod > 1 and [Money] of MyConsumer >= Price

[set [Cons] of MyConsumer [Cons] of MyConsumer + 1

;set [Need] of MyConsumer true

set [Money] of MyConsumer [Money] of MyConsumer - Price

set Sell Sell + 1

set Prod Prod - 1

set Money Money + Price]]]

[set heading random 360 fd vision]]

end
```

The fourth procedure ComputeBalance is used to compute the balance at the end of every time period. If the consumer has a quantity of products Cons higher or equal than one then if Need = false then the value of Cons is decremented with one and the value of Need is set to true.

```
to ComputeBalance

if Need = false and Cons >= 1 [set Cons Cons - 1 set Need true]

end
```

CONFLICT OF INTEREST

The author(s) confirm that this article content has no conflict of interest.

ACKNOWLEDGEMENT

Declared none.

REFERENCES

Axelrod, R. M. (1997). Advancing the Art of Simulation in the Social Sciences. In Conte R., & Hegselmann, R., Terna P. (Eds.). *Simulating Social Phenomena, Lecture Notes in Economics and Mathematical Systems. 456*, 21-40. Berlin: Springer-Verlag

Axtell, R. L. & Epstein, J. M. (1994). Agent-based Modeling: Understanding Our Creations. *The Bulletin of the Santa Fe Institute.* Winter, 28-32

Christley, S., & Xiang, X. Madey, G. (2004). Ontology for agent-based modeling and simulation. In Macal C. M., & Sallach, D., North, M. J. (Eds.). (2004) *Proceedings of the Agent 2004 Conference on Social Dynamics: Interaction, Reflexivity and Emergence.* Chicago, IL: Argonne National Laboratory and The University of Chicago. http://www.agent2005.anl.gov/Agent2004.pdf

Drogoul, A., & Vanbergue, D., Meurisse, T. (2003). Multi-Agent Based Simulation: Where are the Agents?. In Sichman, J. S., & Bousquet, F., Davidsson, P. (Eds.). *Proceedings of MABS 2002 Multi-Agent-Based Simulation, Lecture Notes in Computer Science. 2581*, 1-15. Bologna, Italy: Springer-Verlag

Edmonds, B. (2001). The Use of Models - making MABS actually work. In Moss, S. & Davidsson, P. (Eds.). *Multi-Agent-Based Simulation, Lecture Notes in Artificial Intelligence 1979.* 15-32. Berlin: Springer-Verlag

Gilbert, N. (2007). *Agent-Based Models. Quantitative Applications in the Social Sciences.* London: SAGE Publications.

Gruber, T. R. (1993). A translation approach to portable ontology specifications. *Knowledge Acquisition. 5*(2), 199-220

Izquierdo, L. R. & Polhill, J. G. (2006). Is your model susceptible to floating point errors?. *Journal of Artificial Societies and Social Simulation. 9*(4), http://jasss.soc.surrey.ac.uk/9/4/4.html.

Kleijnen, J. P. C. (1995). Verification and validation of simulation models. *European Journal of Operational Research. 82*(1), 145-162.

Moss, S., & Edmonds, B., Wallis, S. (1997). Validation and Verification of Computational Models with Multiple Cognitive Agents. *Centre for Policy Modelling Report. 97-25*, http://cfpm.org/cpmrep25.html.

Pignotti, E., & Edwards, P., Preece, A., Polhill, J. G, Gotts, N. M. (2005) Semantic support for computational land-use modelling. *5th International Symposium on Cluster Computing and the Grid (CCGRID 2005).* 840-847. Piscataway, NJ: IEEE Press.

Polhill, J. G. & Gotts, N. M. (2006). A new approach to modelling frameworks. *Proceedings of the First World Congress on Social Simulation.* 50-57. Kyoto.

Polhill, J. G., & Izquierdo, L. R., Gotts, N. M. (2005a). The ghost in the model (and other effects of floating point arithmetic). *Journal of Artificial Societies and Social Simulation. 8*(1) http://jasss.soc.surrey.ac.uk/8/1/5.html.

Polhill, J. G. & Izquierdo, L. R. (2005b). Lessons learned from converting the artificial stock market to interval arithmetic. *Journal of Artificial Societies and Social Simulation. 8*(2), http://jasss.soc.surrey.ac.uk/8/2/2.html.

Polhill, J. G., & Izquierdo, L. R., Gotts, N. M. (2006). What every agent-based modeller should know about floating point arithmetic. *Environmental Modelling & Software.* 21(3), 283-309

Polhill, J. G., & Pignotti, E., Gotts, N. M, Edwards, P., Preece, A. (2007). A Semantic Grid Service for Experimentation with an Agent-Based Model of Land-Use Change. *Journal of Artificial Societies and Social Simulation. 10*(2), http://jasss.soc.surrey.ac.uk/10/2/2.html.

Richiardi, M., & Leombruni, R., Saam, N. J., Sonnessa, M. (2006). A Common Protocol for Agent-Based Social Simulation. *Journal of Artificial Societies and Social Simulation.* 9(1), http://jasss.soc.surrey.ac.uk/9/1/15.html.

Sansores, C., & Pavón, J. (2005). Agent-based simulation replication: A model driven architecture approach. In Gelbukh, A. F., & de Albornoz, A., Terashima-Marín, H. (Eds.). *MICAI 2005: Advances in Artificial Intelligence, 4th Mexican International Conference on Artificial Intelligence, Monterrey, Mexico, November 14-18, 2005, Proceedings. Lecture Notes in Computer Science.* 3789, 244-253. Berlin Heidelberg: Springer.

Sargent, R. G. (2003). Verification and Validation of Simulation Models. In Chick S, Sánchez P J, Ferrin D, and Morrice, D. J., (Eds.). *Proceedings of the 2003 Winter Simulation Conference.* 37-48. Piscataway, NJ: IEEE.

Stanislaw, H. (1986). Tests of computer simulation validity. What do they measure?. *Simulation and Games. 17*, 173-191

Taylor, A. J. (1983). The Verification of Dynamic Simulation Models. *Journal of the Operational Research Society, 34*(3), 233-242

Wilensky, U. (1999). *NetLogo.* http://ccl.northwestern.edu/netlogo/. Center for Connected Learning and Computer-Based Modeling. Evanston, IL: Northwestern University

Send Orders of Reprints at bspsaif@emirates.net.ae

CHAPTER 4

The Computational Experiments

Abstract: In this chapter, we perform five computer experiments that simulate the functioning of the artificial economy with different values for the three control parameters: rs={-2,-1,0,1,2}, NoProducers={1,2,3,.,100}, and NoConsumers={1,2,3,.,100}. Based on these five experiments, we measure five indexes: Herfindahl-Hirschman index, Gini index, mean value of prices for products, mean value of prices for resources, and mean value of obtained production.

Keywords: Computer experiments, Herfindahl-Hirschman index, Gini index, composite index that measure economy performance.

In the scientific context, a computational experiment or a computer experiment refers to mathematical modeling using computer simulation and typically implies two phases. The modeling phase and the experimentation phase (Sacks *et al.* 1989). In such experiment a computer model is used to make inferences about a system. The computer model takes the place of an experiment we cannot do. Under these circumstances, the phrase *in silico* experiment is used (Sieburg, 1990).

Computational experiments can be seen as a branch of applied statistics, because the user must take into account the next sources of uncertainty:

(i)   First, the models may contain parameters whose values are not certain (are random);

(ii) Second, the models themselves are imperfect representations of the studied system;

(iii) Third, data collected from the system that might be used to calibrate the models are imperfectly measured.

However, most practitioners of computational experiments do not see themselves as statisticians (Santner *et al.* 2003). Experimentation to study complex systems can be conducted at different levels of accuracy or sophistication. Complex mathematical models, implemented in large computer codes, are used as a tool to study such systems. Doing the corresponding physical experiments would be costly (Reese *et al.* 2004).

Study of multiple computational experiments involves two aspects:

(i)   Experimental planning;

(ii) Analysis and modeling of experimental results (Kennedy *et al.* 2000).

The main reason of a simulation project is to run your model(s) and to try to understand the results. To do so effectively, you need to plan ahead before doing the runs, since just trying different things to see what happens can be a very inefficient way of attempting to learn about your models or systems behaviours. Careful planning of your experiments will generally give you positive results in terms of how effectively you learn about the system(s) and how you can develop your model(s) further - see (Law *et al.* 1991; Kelton *et al.* 2002; Banks *et al.* 1996; Kleijnen, 1998; Hood *et al.* 1992; Swain *et al.* 1994; Kelton, 1997).

PLANNING OF COMPUTER EXPERIMENTS

In this chapter we are going to make an operational validation of the model described in previous chapters of this eBook. Operational validation will check how the model performs during running a set of computer experiments in the frame of NetLogo software platform using our personal experience in using the Behaviour Space tool located in Tools menu of NetLogo interface (Damaceanu, 2007; Damaceanu 2008a; Damaceanu 2008b; Damaceanu, 2010; Damaceanu, 2010; Damaceanu, 2011a; Damaceanu, 2011b; Damaceanu, 2011c; Damaceanu *et al.* 2012). We will do 5 computer experiments described in Table **1** (Wilensky, 1999).

Table 1: Description of computer experiments

Name	Description
E1	This experiment has 10000 runs with the following control parameters rs=0, NoProducers={1,2,3,.,100}, and NoConsumers={1,2,3,.,100}. The runs measure: Herfindahl-Hirschman index MeanH, Gini index MeanG, mean value of prices for products MeanP, mean value of prices for resources MeanR, and mean value of obtained production TotalS.
E2	This experiment has 10000 runs with the following control parameters rs=-1, NoProducers={1,2,3,.,100}, and NoConsumers={1,2,3,.,100}. The runs measure: Herfindahl-Hirschman index MeanH, Gini index MeanG, mean value of prices for products MeanP, mean value of prices for resources MeanR, and mean value of obtained production TotalS.

Table 1: contd…

E3	This experiment has 10000 runs with the following control parameters rs=1, NoProducers={1,2,3,.,100}, and NoConsumers={1,2,3,.,100}. The runs measure: Herfindahl-Hirschman index MeanH, Gini index MeanG, mean value of prices for products MeanP, mean value of prices for resources MeanR, and mean value of obtained production TotalS.
E4	This experiment has 10000 runs with the following control parameters rs=-2, NoProducers={1,2,3,.,100}, and NoConsumers={1,2,3,.,100}. The runs measure: Herfindahl-Hirschman index MeanH, Gini index MeanG, mean value of prices for products MeanP, mean value of prices for resources MeanR, and mean value of obtained production TotalS.
E5	This experiment has 10000 runs with the following control parameters rs=2, NoProducers={1,2,3,.,100}, and NoConsumers={1,2,3,.,100}. The runs measure: Herfindahl-Hirschman index MeanH, Gini index MeanG, mean value of prices for products MeanP, mean value of prices for resources MeanR, and mean value of obtained production TotalS.

Figure 1: The Behaviour Space tool located in Tools menu.

These 5 computer experiments are run using the Behaviour Space tool located in Tools menu of NetLogo interface – see (Fig. **1**). If you select this option on the computer screen will appear the BahaviorSpace window. In this window, there is a list of computer experiments - see (Fig. **2**). You must select one of them and after this selection you can press Run button. If you pressed this button, then a new window will appear on the screen asking you to select in which type of format do you want to save the simulation results - see (Fig. **3**). You must select

Table option and after it, you can press OK button and a new window is on the computer screen asking you to enter the name of the file that will store the simulation results (E1.csv) –see (Fig. **4**). After you entered the name of the file, then press Save button and the simulation will start – see (Fig. **5**).

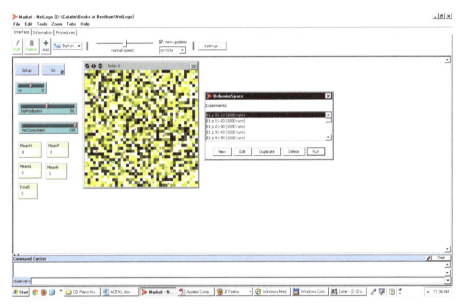

Figure 2: The Behaviour Space window.

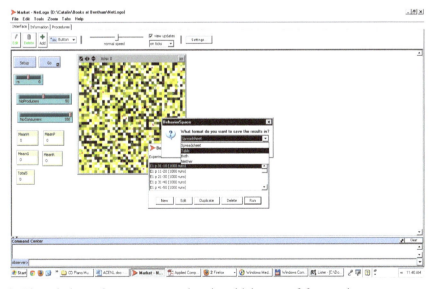

Figure 3: The window where you can select in which type of format do you want to save the simulation results.

The same procedure must be followed for the other four experiments (E2-E6). The results of these computer experiments are stored in Comma Separated Values (CSV) files. This is a plain-text data format that is readable by any text editor as well as by most popular spreadsheet and database programs – see (Figs. **6** and **7**).

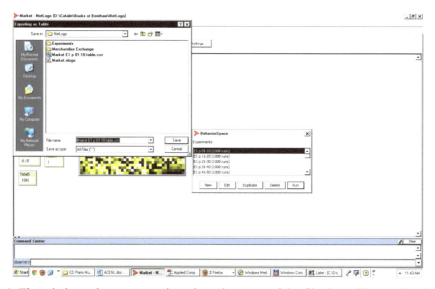

Figure 4: The window where you can introduce the name of the file that will store the simulation results.

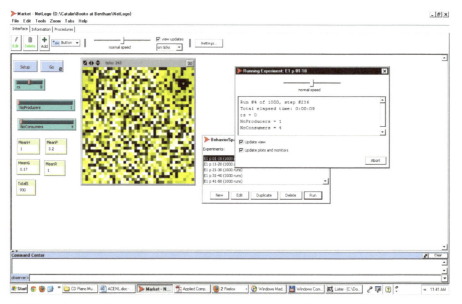

Figure 5: The window where you can see your computer experiment running.

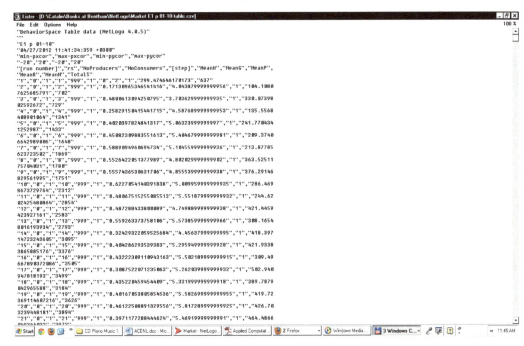

Figure 6: The plain text data format of E1.csv file.

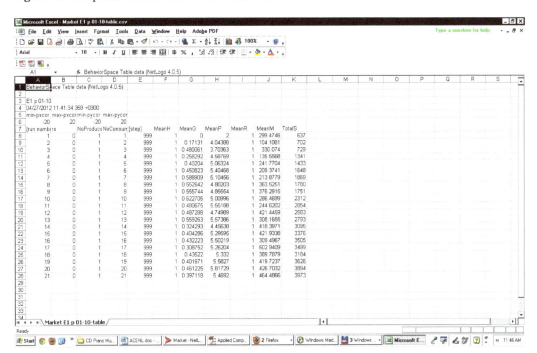

Figure 7: The results of computational experiment E1 stored in E1.csv file are readable using Microsoft Excel.

THE RESULTS OF COMPUTER EXPERIMENTS

The results obtained after running experiments E1-5 are described in detail in Appendix 1. Every computer experiment has a number of 10000 runs for rs={0,-1,1,-2,2}, i consumers and j producers, where i = {1,2,3,..,100}, and j ={1,2,3,..,100}. These experiments measure the following indexes:

- The value of Herfindahl-Hirschman index MeanH (h_{ij});

- The value of Gini index MeanG (g_{ij});

- The mean value of prices for products MeanP (p_{ij});

- The mean value of prices for resources MeanR (r_{ij});

- The mean value of obtained production TotalS (y_{ij}).

Based on the results presented in Appendix 1, we computed the following means and rates (where rate is value that range from 0 that is very bad rate to 1 which is an excellent rate):

- $$h_j = \frac{\sum\limits_{i=1}^{100} h_{ij}}{100}, \quad R_j(h) = \frac{h_{max} - h_j}{h_{max} - h_{min}},$$ where h_j is the mean value of Herfindahl-Hirschman index obtained in the case when there are j producers, $R_j(h)$ is the rate obtained for Herfindahl-Hirschman index, h_{max} and h_{min} are maximum and minimum value of h_j - see (Fig. **8**);

- $$g_j = \frac{\sum\limits_{i=1}^{100} g_{ij}}{100}, \quad R_j(g) = \frac{g_{max} - g_j}{g_{max} - g_{min}},$$ where g_j is the mean value of Gini index obtained in the case when there are j producers, $R_j(g)$ is the rate obtained for Gini index, g_{max} and g_{min} are maximum and minimum value of g_j - see (Fig. **9**);

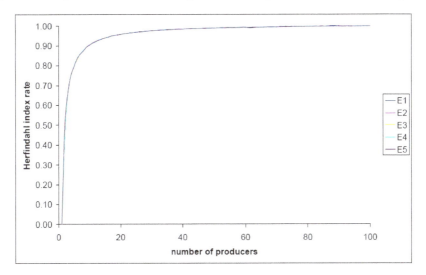

Figure 8: Herfindahl-Hirschman rate.

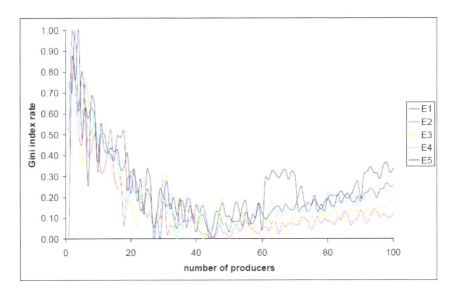

FIgure 9: Gini rate.

- $p_j = \dfrac{\displaystyle\sum_{i=1}^{100} p_{ij}}{100}$, $R_j(p) = \dfrac{p_{max} - p_j}{p_{max} - p_{min}}$, where p_j is the mean value of prices for products obtained in the case when there are j producers, $R_j(p)$ is the rate obtained for prices of products, where p_{max} and p_{min} are maximum and minimum value of p_j - see (Fig. **10**);

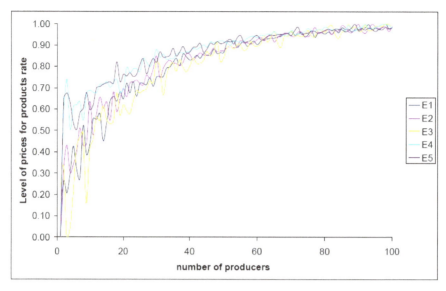

Figure 10: The evolution of level of prices rate.

- $$r_j = \frac{\sum\limits_{i=1}^{100} r_{ij}}{100}, \quad R_j(r) = \frac{r_{max} - r_j}{r_{max} - r_{min}},$$ where r_j is the mean value of prices for resources obtained in the case when there are j producers, $R_j(r)$ is the rate obtained for prices of resources, where r_{max} and r_{min} are maximum and minimum value of r_j - see (Fig. **11**);

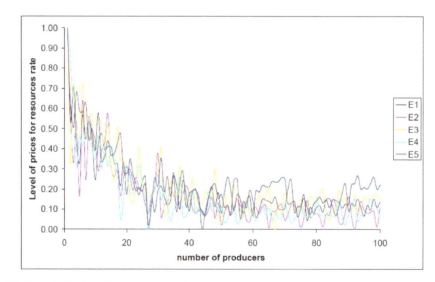

Figure 11: Level of prices for resources rate.

-   $y_j = \dfrac{\sum\limits_{i=1}^{100} y_{ij}}{100}$, $R_j(y) = \dfrac{y_j - y_{min}}{y_{max} - y_{min}}$, where y_j is the mean value of

production obtained in the case when there are j producers, $R_j(y)$ is the rate obtained for obtained production, where y_{max} and y_{min} are maximum and minimum value of y_j - see (Fig. **12**).

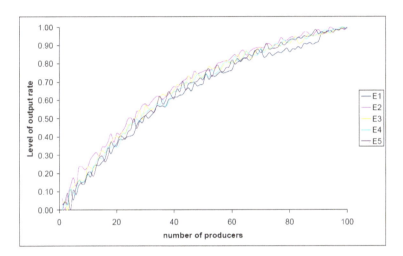

Figure 12: Level of output rate.

CONFLICT OF INTEREST

The author(s) confirm that this article content has no conflict of interest.

ACKNOWLEDGEMENT

Declared none.

REFERENCES

Banks, J., Carson, J.S., Nelson, B.L. (1996). *Discrete event system simulation.* 2d ed. Upper Saddle River, N.J.: Prentice-Hall

Damaceanu, R.C., (2007). Using Netlogo in the training-learning process of Social Sciences. Analele Stiintifice ale Universitatii " Alexandru Ioan Cuza" - Sect. Stiintele Educatiei, 11, 55-64

Damaceanu, R.C. (2008a). An agent-based computational study of wealth distribution in function of resource growth interval using NetLogo. *Applied Mathematics and Computation*, 201, 371-377

Damaceanu, R.C. (2008b). A comparative analysis of three multiagent computational algorithms used to Harvest grain. *Lucrari Stiintifice - Seria Agronomie*, 51, 186-191

Damaceanu, R.C. (2010). A Multi-Agent Computational Model of Trade. *Year-Book „Petre Andrei" University from Iasi, Fascicle: Law, Economic Sciences, Political Sciences - THE IMPLICATIONS OF GLOBAL FINANCIAL AND ECONOMIC CRISIS ON THE ROMANIAN BUSINESS ENVIRONMENT*, 1, 135-152

Damaceanu, R.C. (2011a). *Agent-based Computational Social Sciences using NetLogo*. Germany: Lambert Academic Publishing

Damaceanu, R.C. (2011b). An Agent-based Computational Study of Wealth Distribution in Function of Technological Progress Using Netlogo. *American Journal of Economics*. 1, 15-20

Damaceanu, R.C. (2011c). *Agent-based Computational Social Sciences using NetLogo*. LAP LAMBERT Academic Publishing.

Damaceanu, R.C., Capraru, B.S., (2012). Implementation of a multi-agent computational model of retail banking market using NetLogo. *Metalurgia International*, 17, 230-235

Hood, S.J., Welch, P.D. (1992). Experimental design issues in simulation with examples from semiconductor manufacturing. In Swain, J.J., Goldsman, D., Crain, R.C., and Wilson, J.R. (ed.). *Proceedings of the 1992 Winter Simulation Conference*. WSC Board of Directors: 255–63.

Kelton, W.D. (1997). Statistical analysis of simulation output. In Andradóttir S, Healy KJ, Withers DH, Nelson BL (eds.). *Proceedings of the 1997 Winter Simulation Conference*. WSC Board of Directors: 23–30.

Kelton, W.D., Sadowski, R.P., Sadowski, D.A. (2002). *Simulation with Arena - 2nd edition*. New York: McGraw-Hill

Kennedy, M.C., O'Hagan, A. (2000). Predicting the output from a complex computer code when fast approximations are available. *Biometrika*. 87: 1-13.

Kleijnen, J.P.C. (1998). Experimental design for sensitivity analysis, optimization, and validation of simulation models. In Banks, J. (ed.). *Handbook of simulation*, New York: John Wiley: 173–223.

Law, A.M., Kelton, W.D. (1991). *Simulation modeling and analysis*. 2nd ed. New York: McGraw-Hill

Reese, C.S., Wilson, A.G., Hamada, M., Martz, H.F., Ryan, K.J. (2004). Integrated analysis of computer and physical experiments. *Technometrics*. 46, 153-164

Sacks J, Welch WJ, Mitchell TJ, Wynn HP, Wynn HP. (1989). Design and Analysis of Computer Experiments. *Statistical Science*. 4(4), 433-435

Santner, T.J., Williams, B.J., Notz, W.I. (2003). *The Design and Analysis of Computer Experiments*. Berlin: Springer

Sieburg, H.B. (1990) Physiological Studies *in silico*. *Studies in the Sciences of Complexity*. 12, 321-342

Swain J.J., Farrington, P.A. (1994) Designing simulation experiments for evaluating manufacturing systems. In Tew, J.D., Manivannan, M.S., Sadowski, D.A., Seila, A.F. (ed.) *Proceedings of the 1994 Winter Simulation Conference*. WSC Board of Directors: 69–76.

Wilensky, U. (1999). *NetLogo*. http://ccl.northwestern.edu/netlogo/. Center for Connected Learning and Computer-Based Modeling. Evanston, IL: Northwestern University

CHAPTER 5

Conclusions

Abstract: In this chapter, we draw the conclusions regarding the evolution of Agent-based Artificial Economy described in Chapter 2, implemented in Chapter 3 using NetLogo, and utilized them for a set of computational experiments in Chapter 4.

Keywords: Global performance of economy, computer experiments.

Global performance (competitiveness) of an economy is a comparative concept of the ability of a economy to sell and supply goods and services in a given market. Although widely used in economics and business management, the usefulness of the concept is vigorously disputed by economists. In recent years, the concept of competitiveness has emerged as a new paradigm in economic development. Competitiveness captures the awareness of both the limitations and challenges posed by global competition, at a time when effective government action is constrained by budgetary constraints and the private sector faces significant barriers to competing in domestic and international markets. The Global Competitiveness Report of the World Economic Forum defines competitiveness as "the set of institutions, policies, and factors that determine the level of productivity of a country" (Schwab, 2009). The term is also used to refer in a broader sense to the economic competitiveness of countries, regions or cities. For example, the way for the European Union to face competitiveness is to invest in education, research, innovation and technological infrastructures (Muldur, 2006; Stajano, 2009).

For our book, in order to study global performance (competitiveness) of an economy based on data obtained after running the five computer experiments, we computed a new composite index pe_j that measures the performance of the economy for j producers using the following formula - see (Fig. **1**):

$$pe_j = (R_j(h)+R_j(g)+R_j(p)+R_j(r)+R_j(y))/5,$$

where:

- $R_j(h) = \dfrac{h_{max} - h_j}{h_{max} - h_{min}}$ is the rate obtained for Herfindahl-Hirschman index, where h_{max} and h_{min} are maximum and minimum value of h_{ij};

$R_j(g) = \dfrac{g_{max} - g_j}{g_{max} - g_{min}}$ is the rate obtained for Gini index, where g_{max} and g_{min} are maximum and minimum value of g_j;

$R_j(p) = \dfrac{p_{max} - p_j}{p_{max} - p_{min}}$ is the rate obtained for prices of products, where p_{max} and p_{min} are maximum and minimum value of p_j;

$R_j(r) = \dfrac{r_{max} - r_j}{r_{max} - r_{min}}$ is the rate obtained for prices of resources, where r_{max} and r_{min} are maximum and minimum value of r_j;

$R_j(y) = \dfrac{y_j - y_{min}}{y_{max} - y_{min}}$ is the rate obtained for obtained production, where y_{max} and y_{min} are maximum and minimum value of y_j.

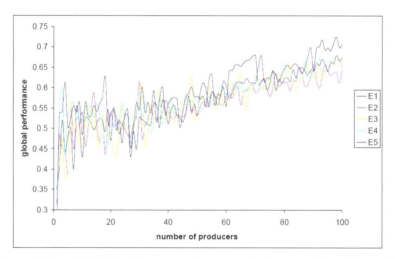

Figure 1: The evolution of global performance of economy in the case of experiments E1-E5.

(Fig. **1**) shows us that the results obtained after running our computer experiments are similar to those observed on real markets, where the most performing economies are those where there are a lot of producers. This conclusion give one more reason for the existence of competition laws that promotes or maintains market competition by regulating anti-competitive conduct of companies (Taylor, 2006).

CONFLICT OF INTEREST

The author(s) confirm that this article content has no conflict of interest.

ACKNOWLEDGEMENT

Declared none.

REFERENCES

Schwab, K. (Ed.) (2009). *World Economic Forum, The Global Competitiveness Report 2009-2010*, SRO-Kundig, http://www3.weforum.org/docs/WEF_GlobalCompetitivenessReport_2009-10.pdf

Muldur, U., *et al.*, (2006). *A New Deal for an Effective European Research Policy*, Springer

Stajano, A. (2009). *Research, Quality, Competitiveness. EU Technology Policy fro the Knowledge-based Society*, Springer

Taylor, M.D. (2006). *International competition law: a new dimension for the WTO?*. Cambridge University Press.

Detailed Results of Computational Experiments

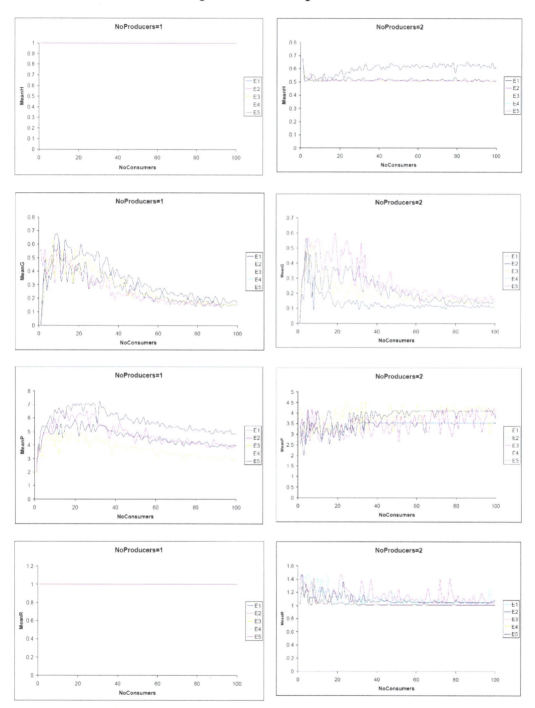

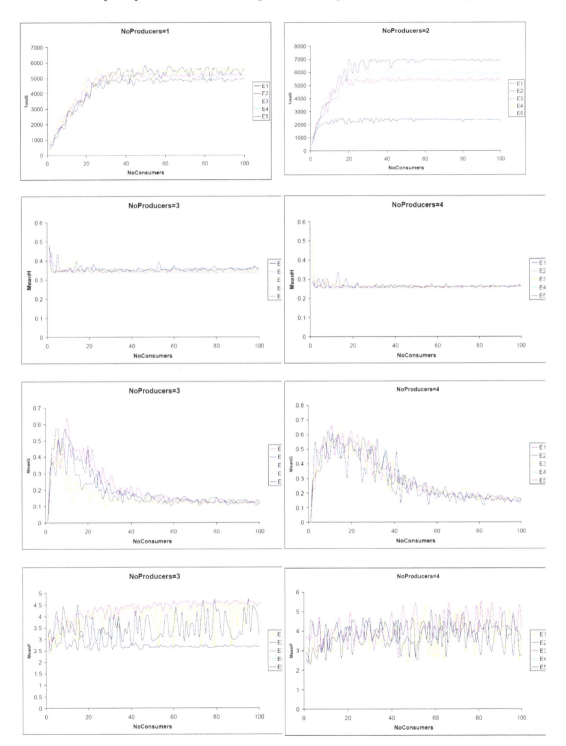

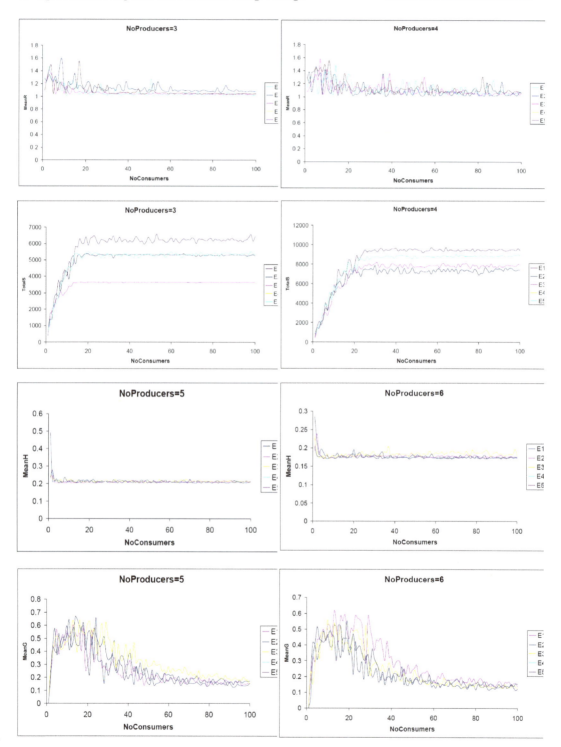

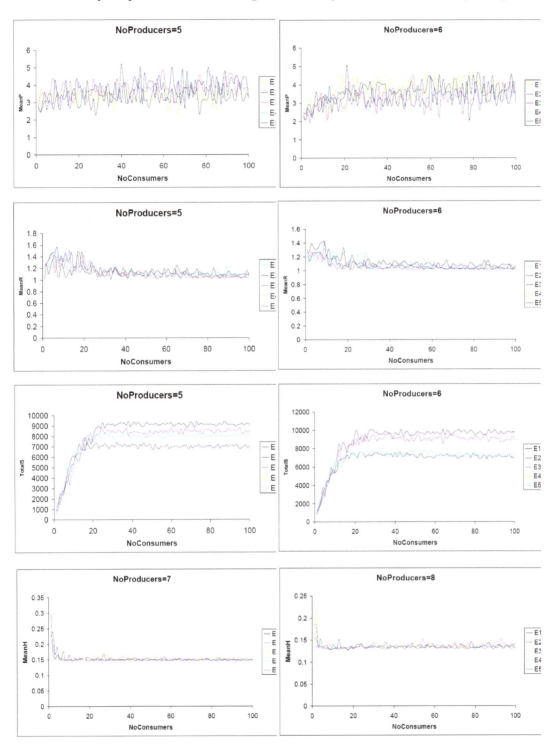

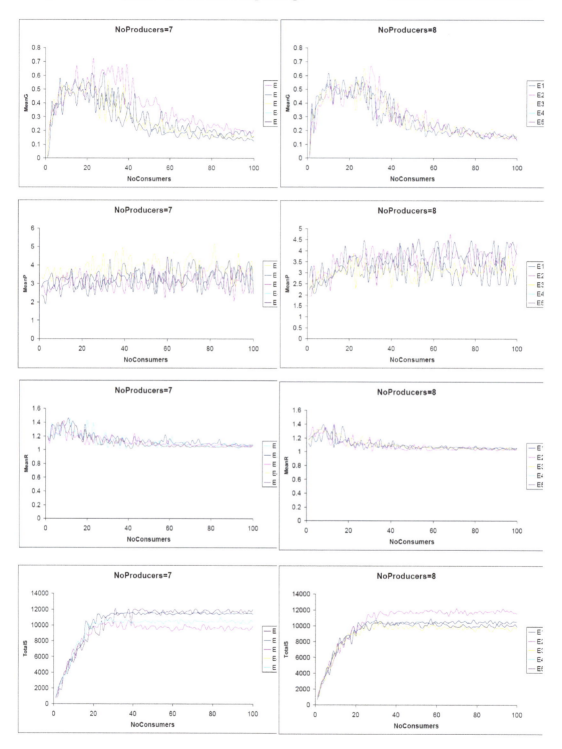

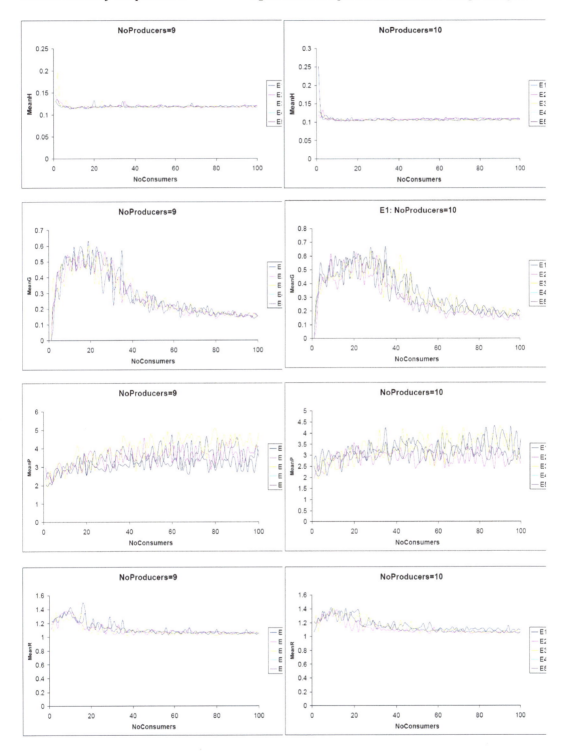

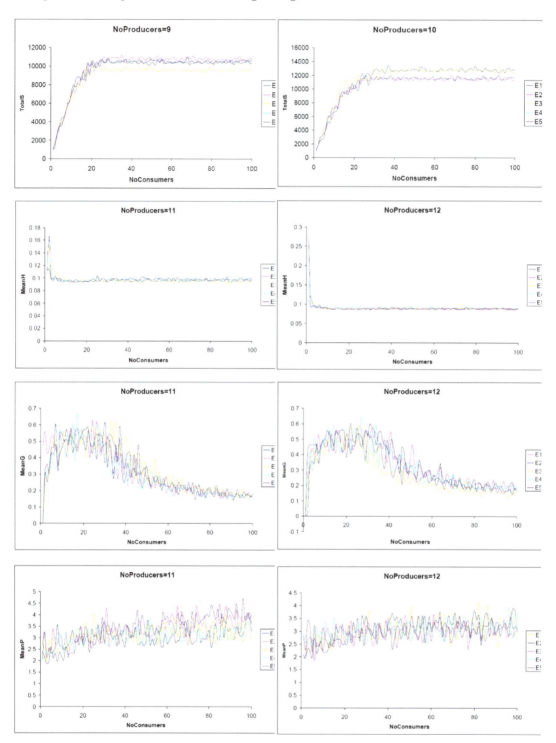

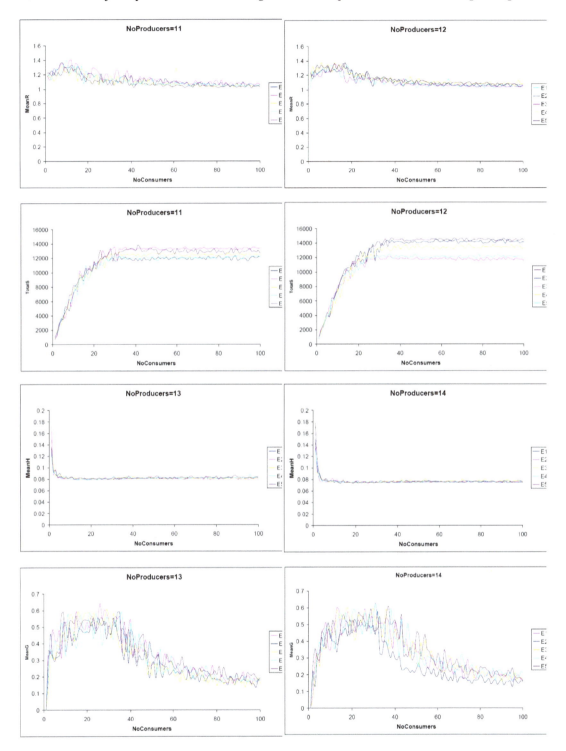

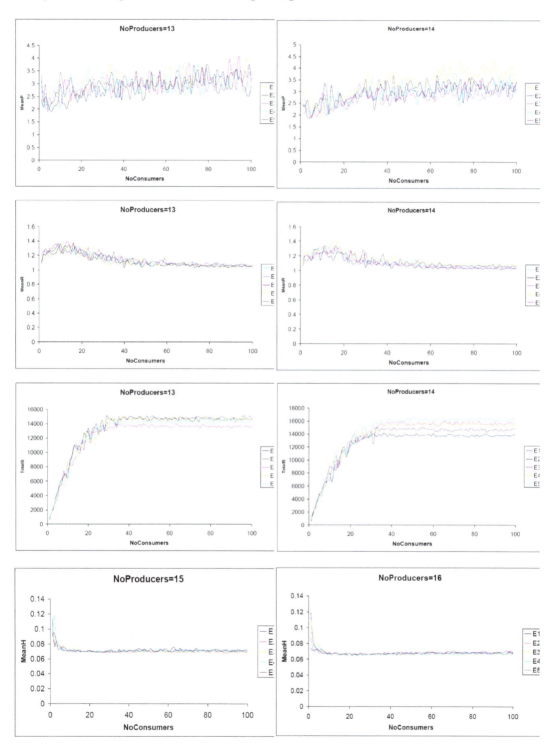

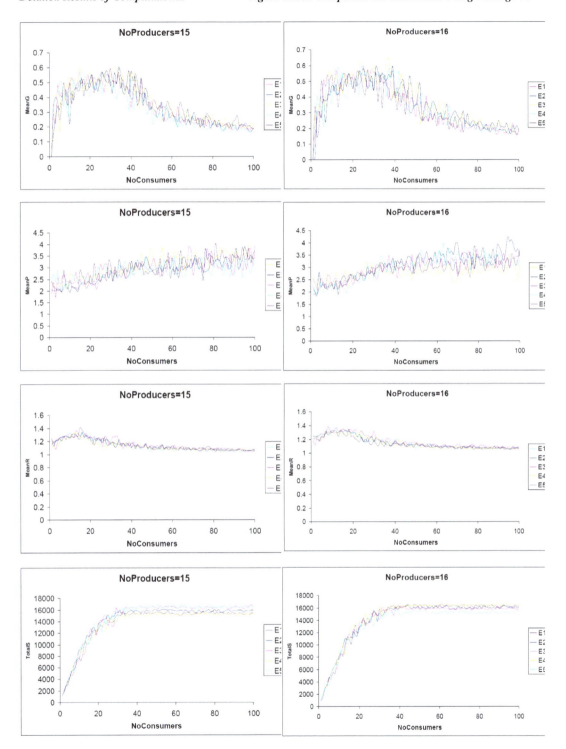

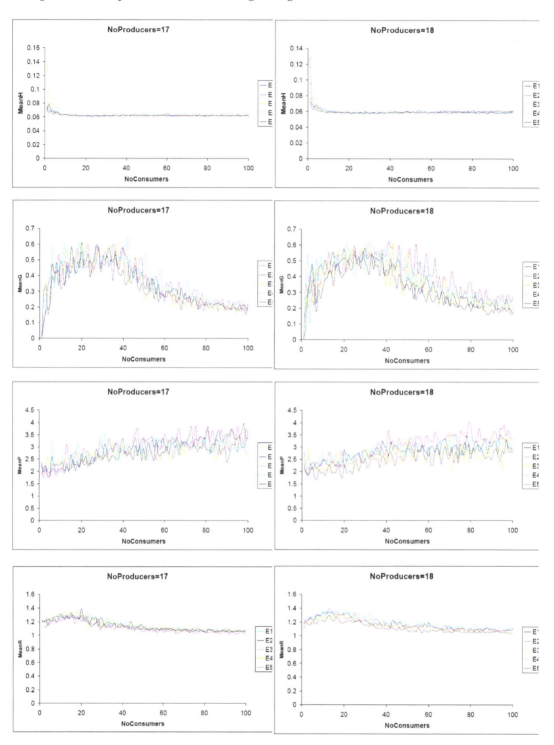

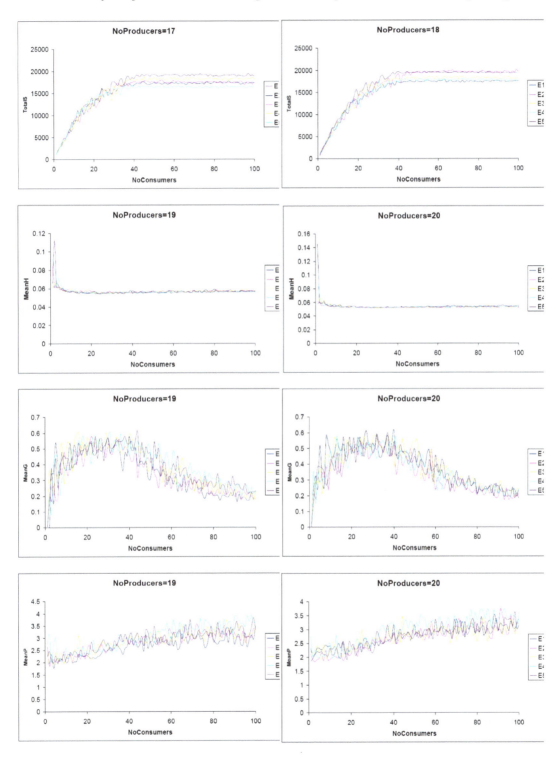

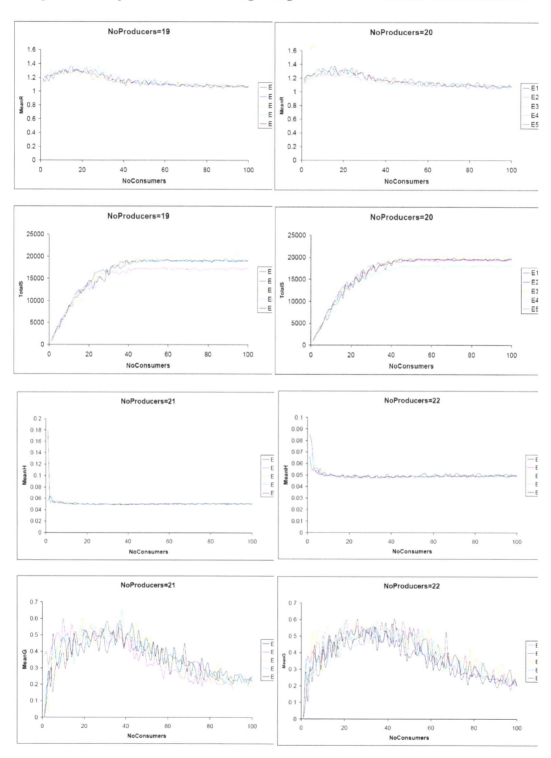

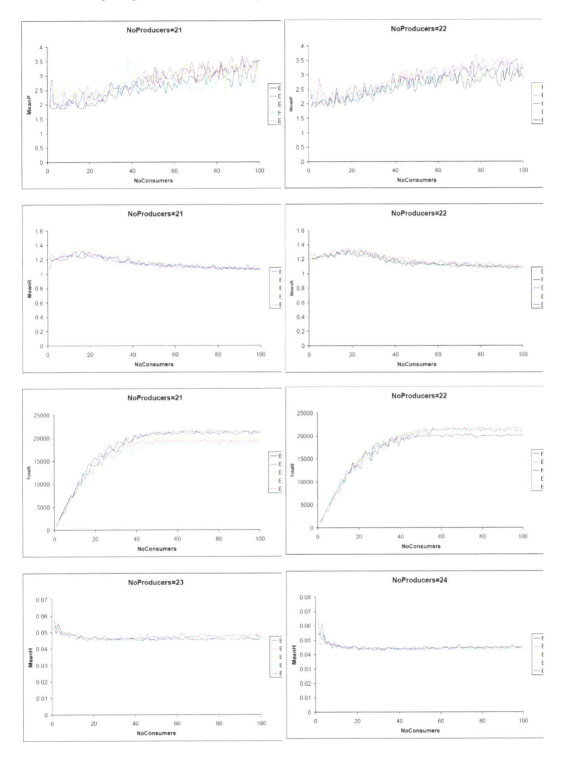

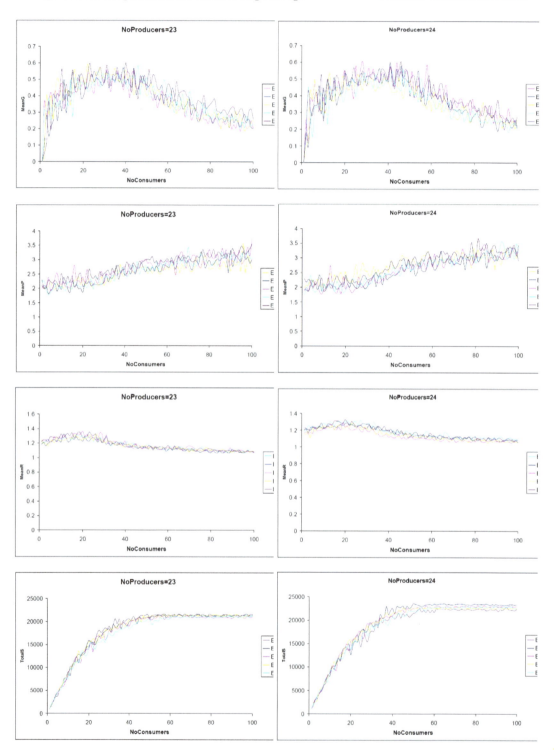

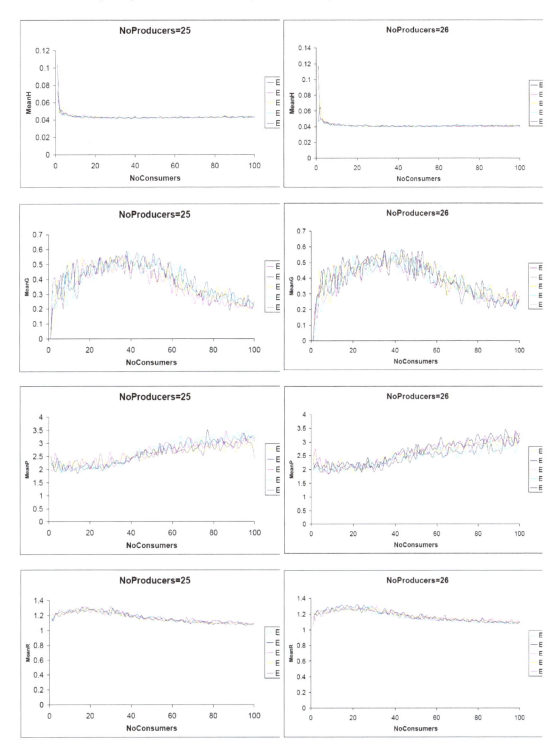

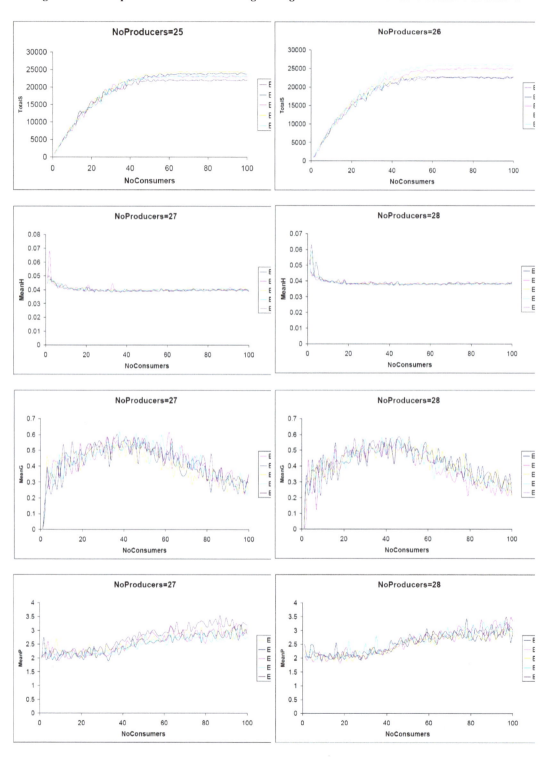

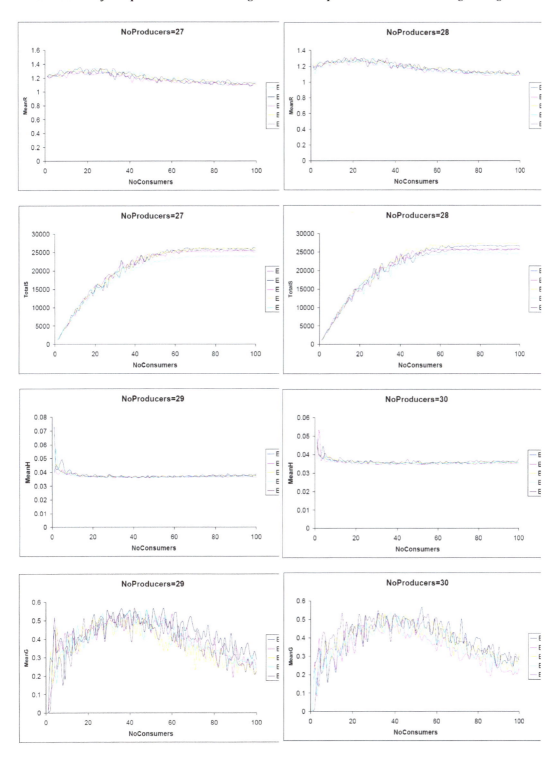

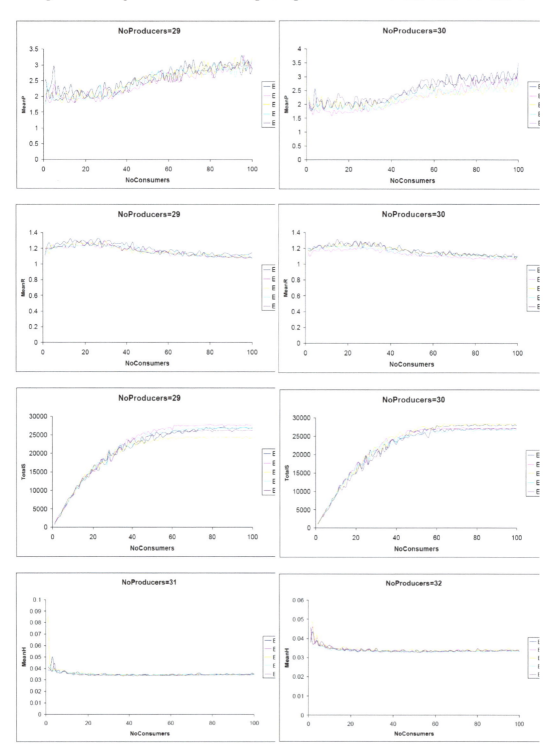

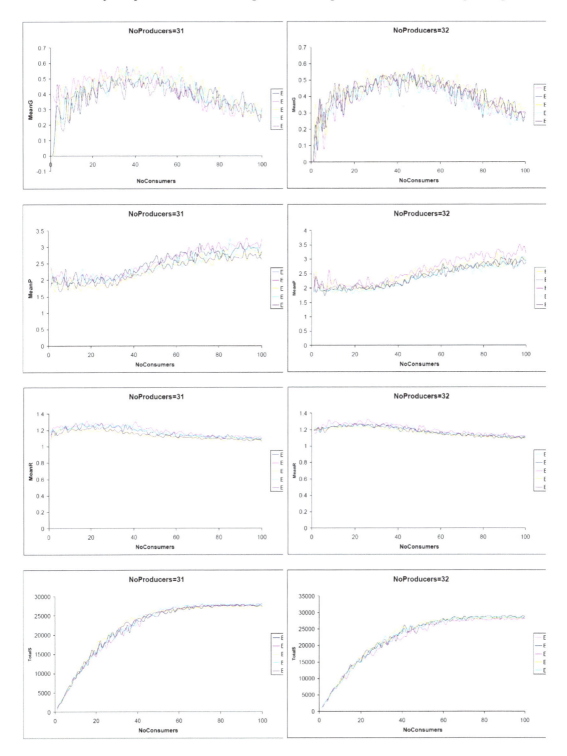

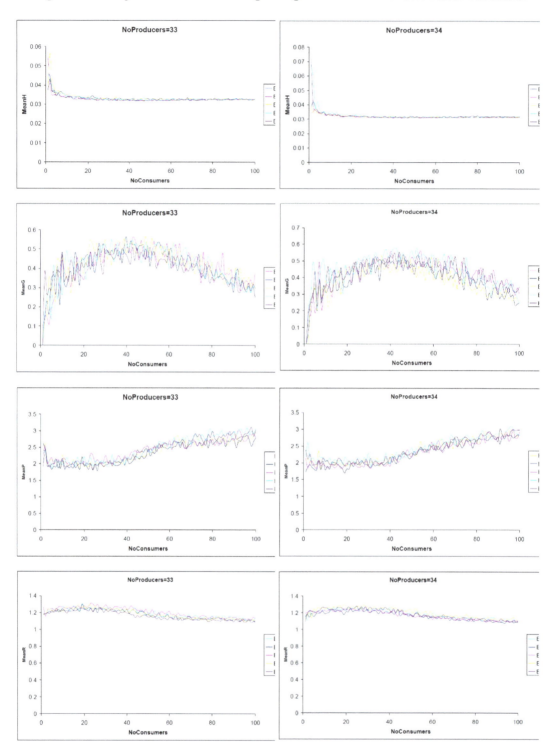

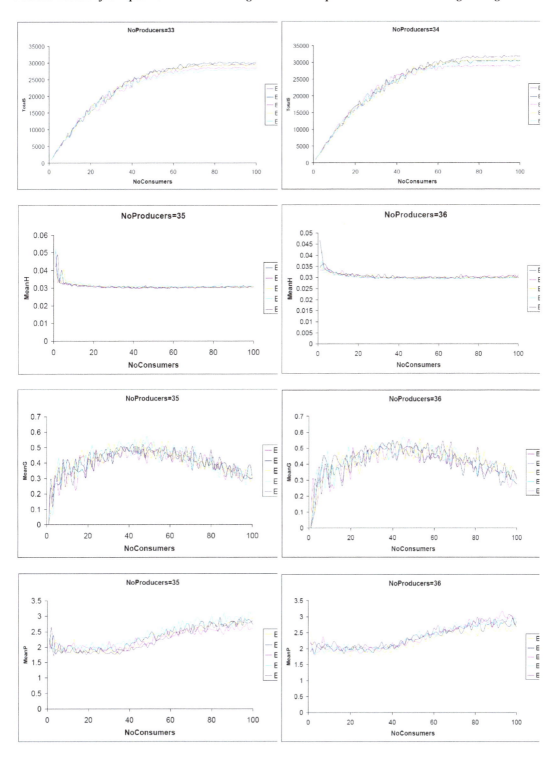

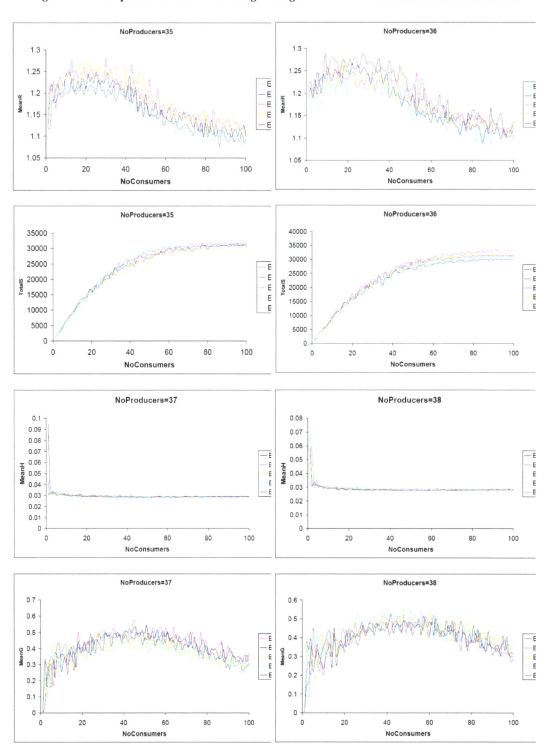

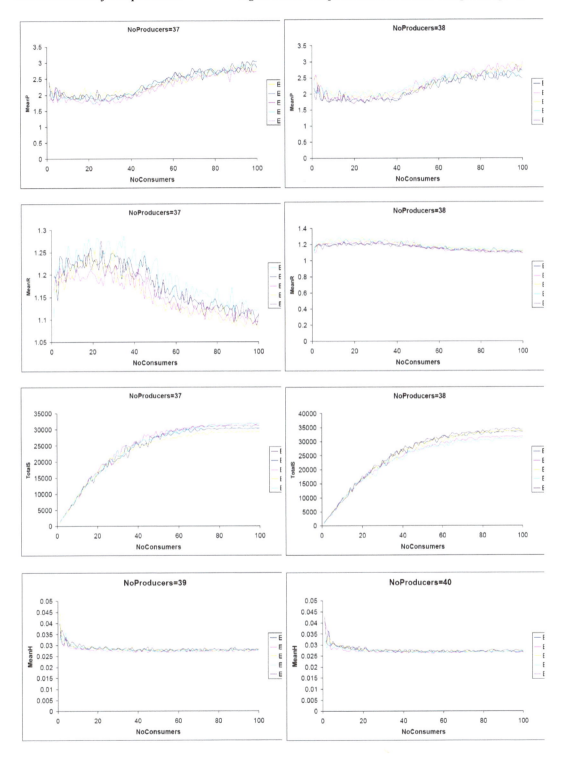

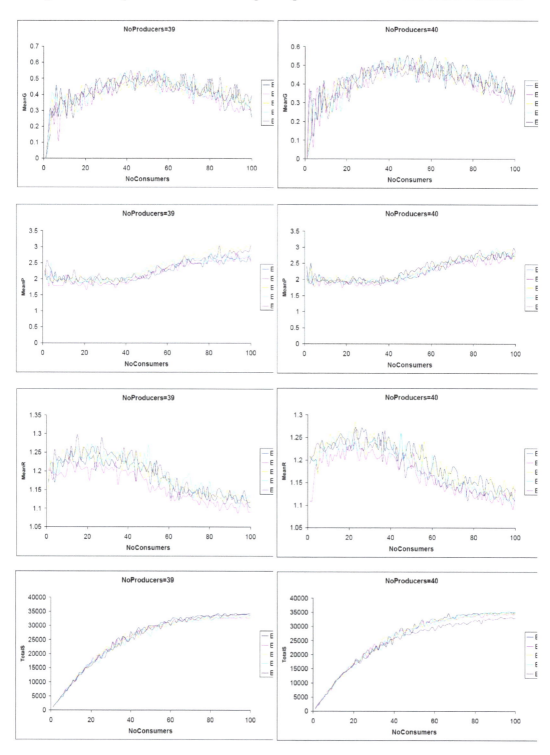

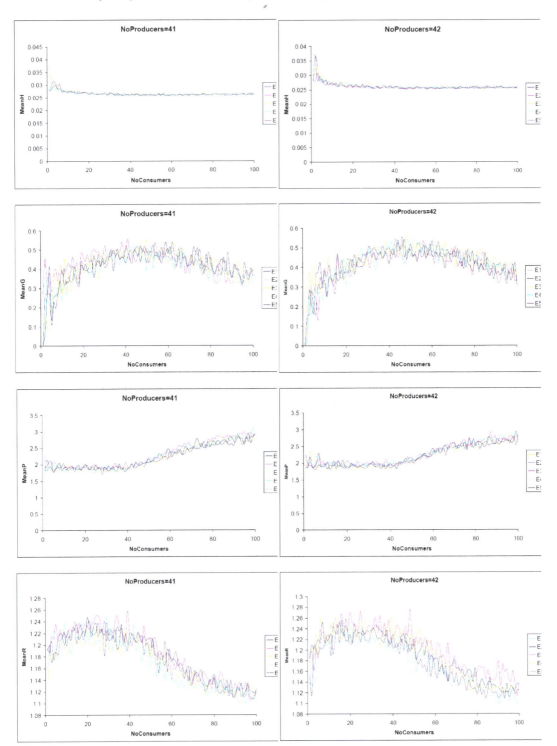

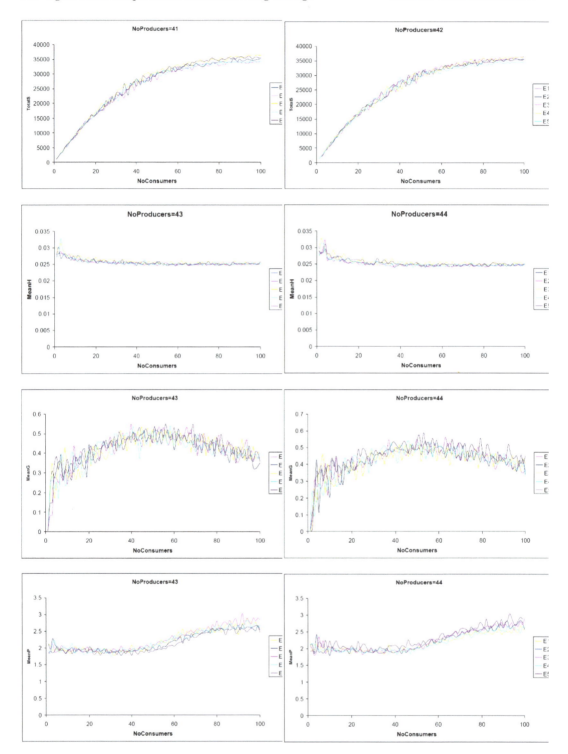

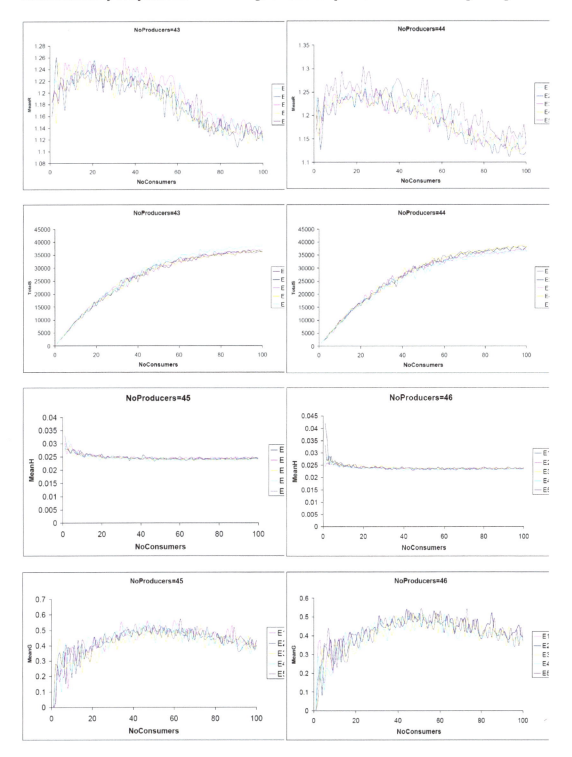

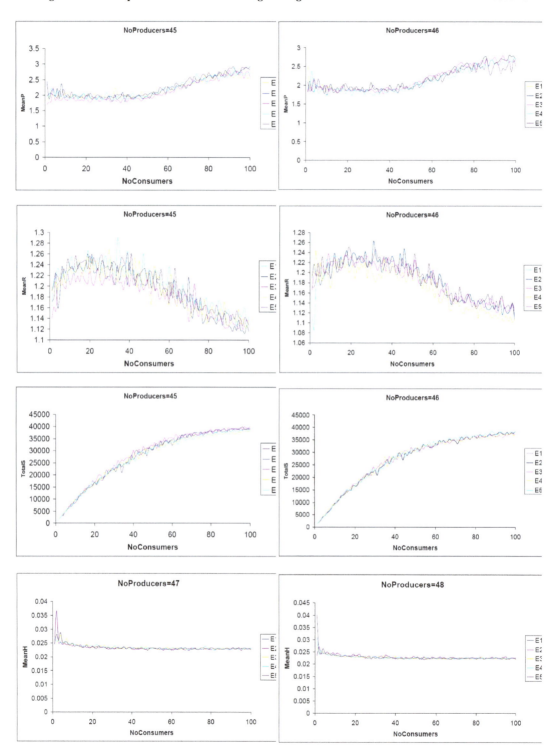

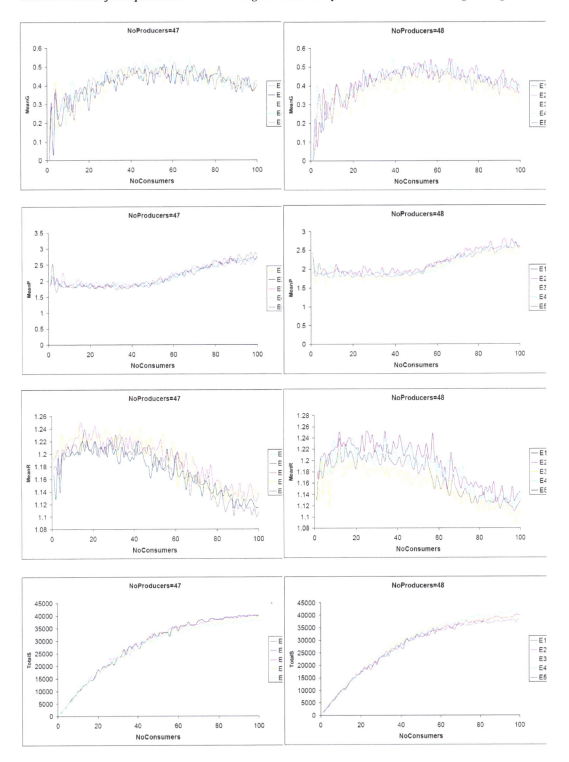

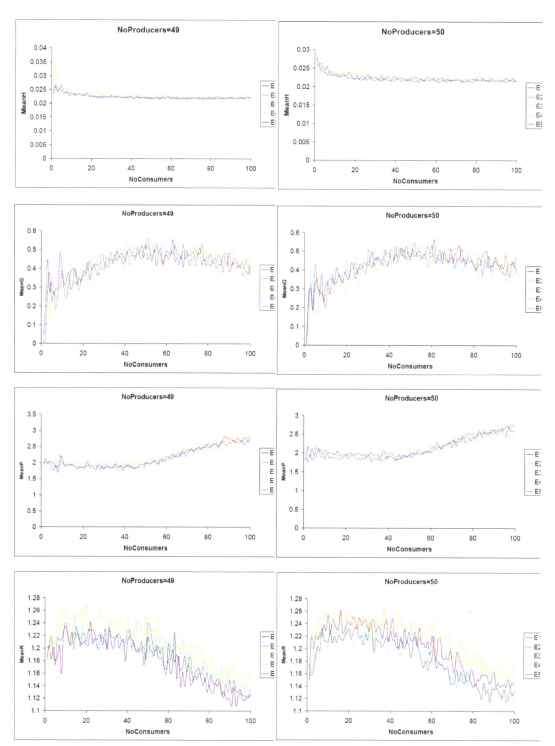

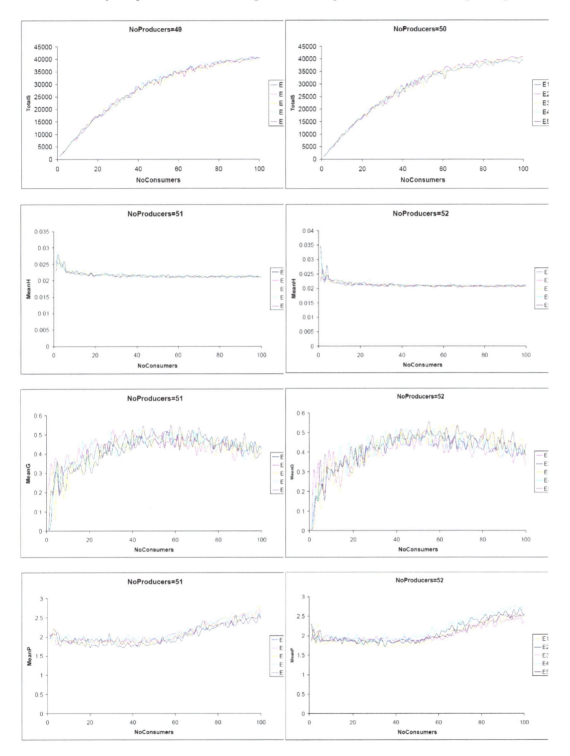

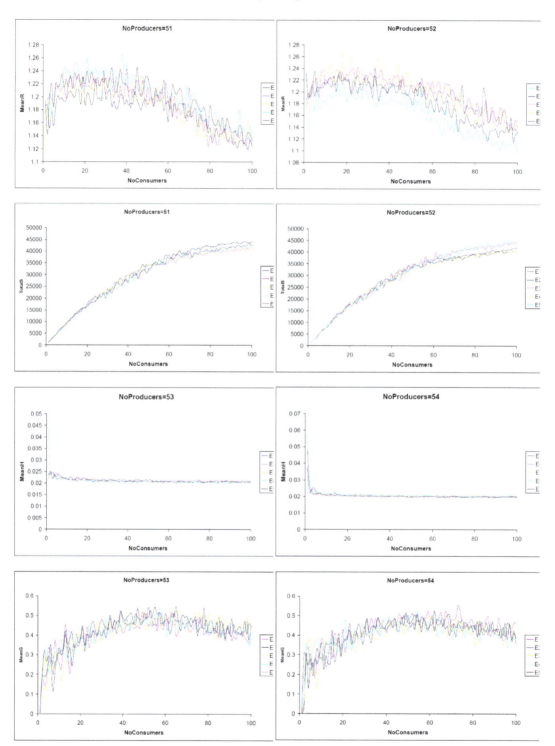

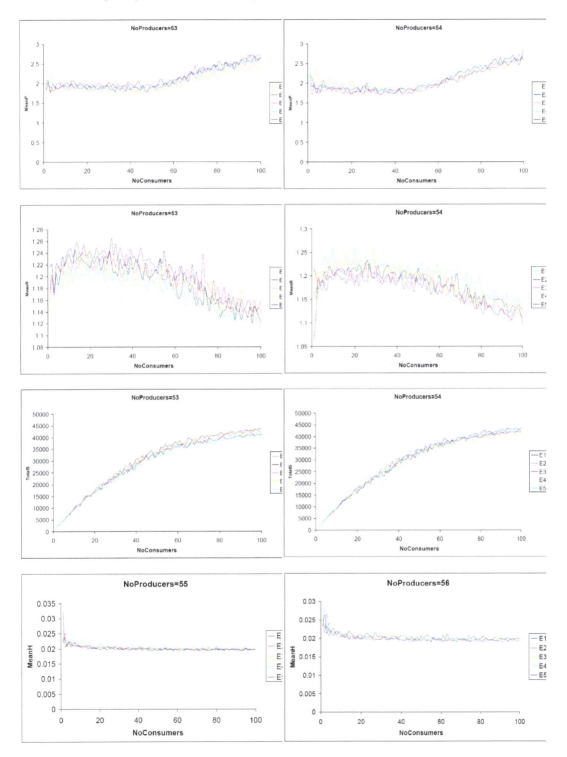

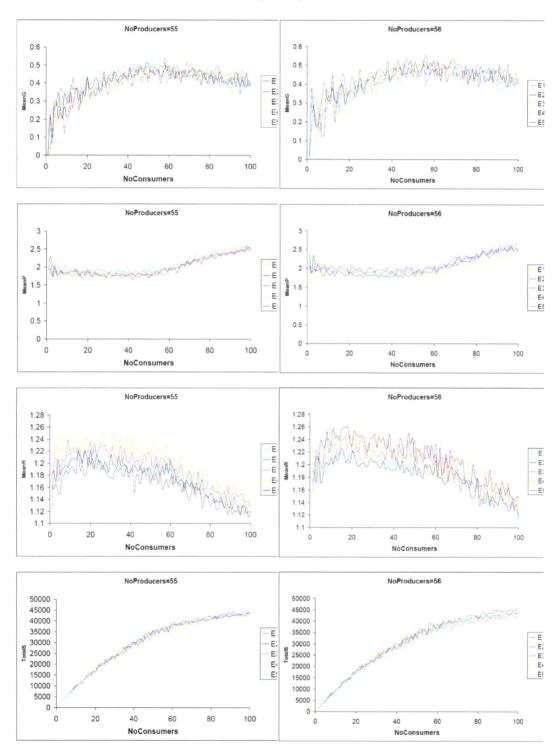

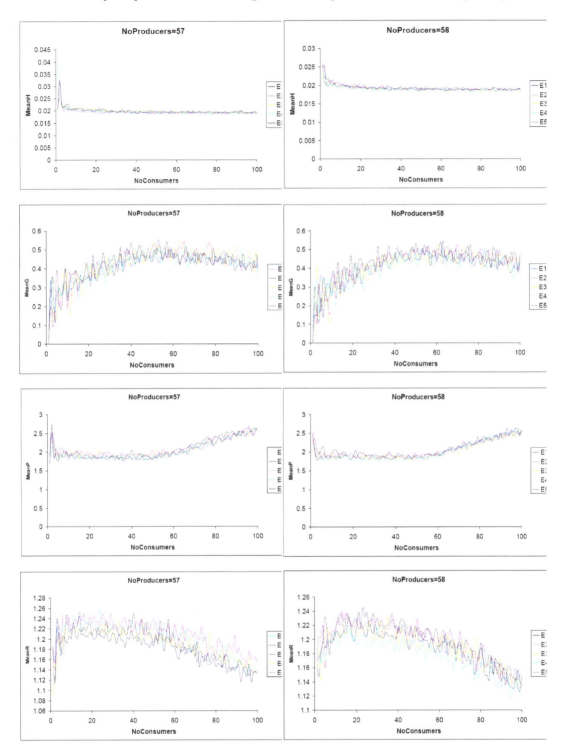

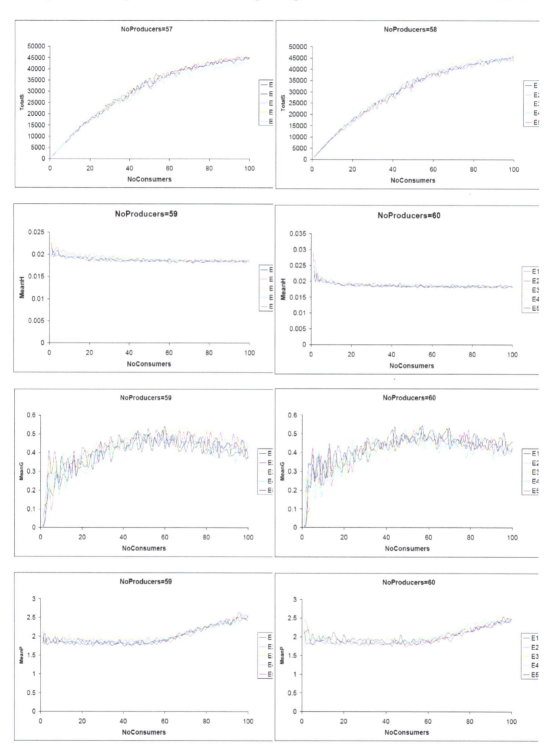

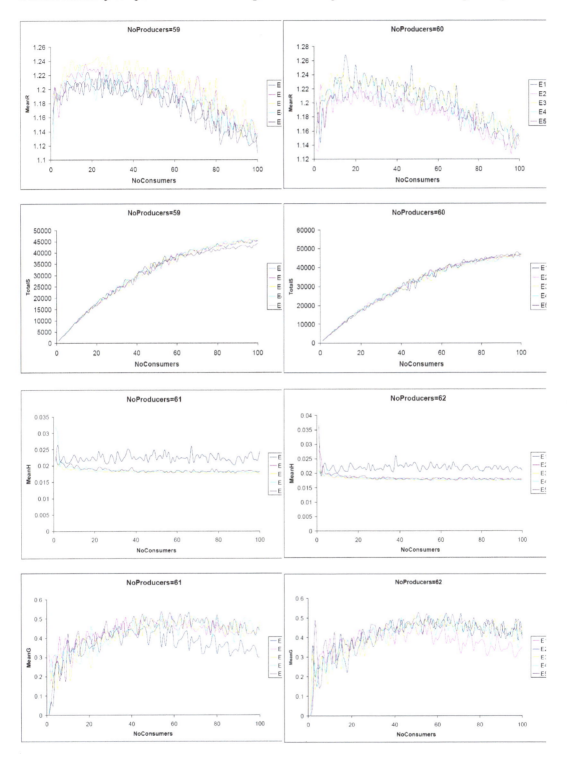

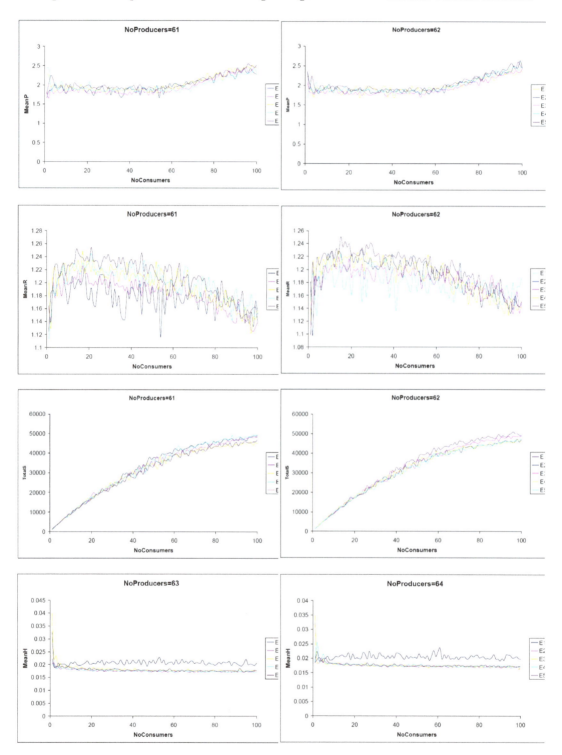

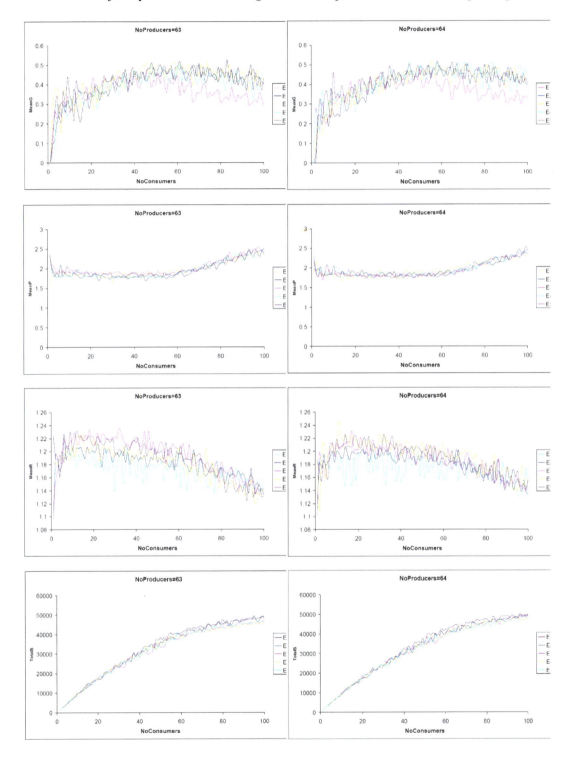

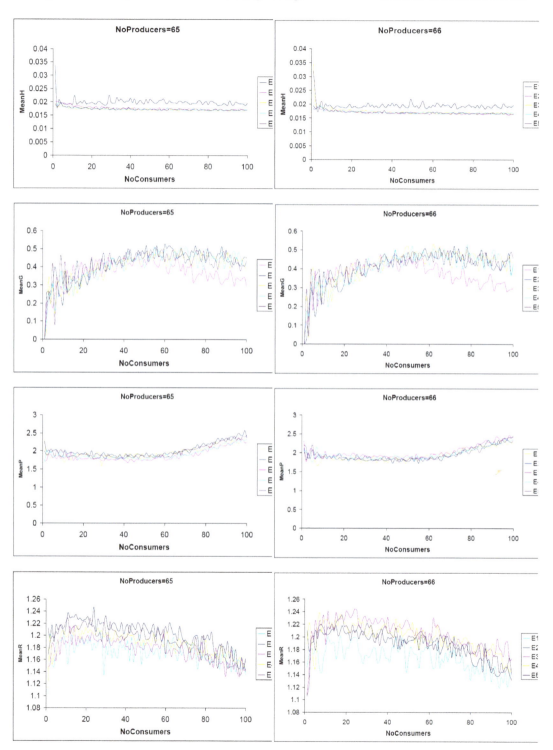

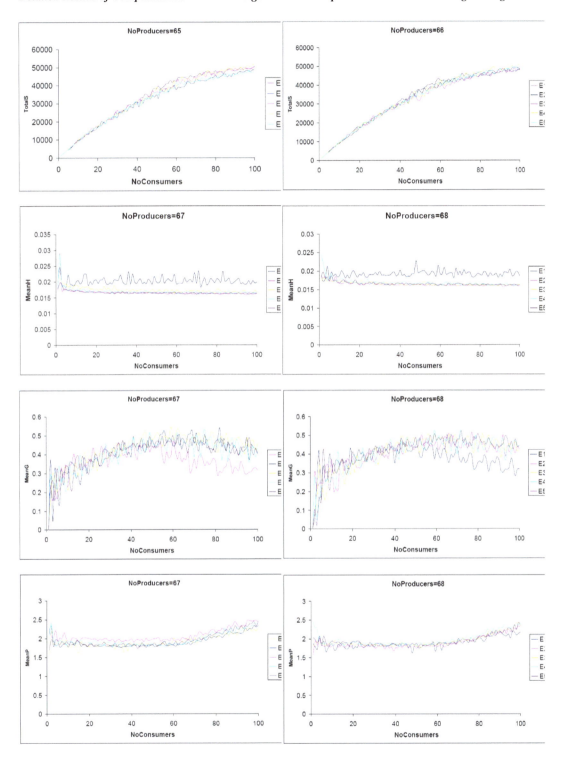

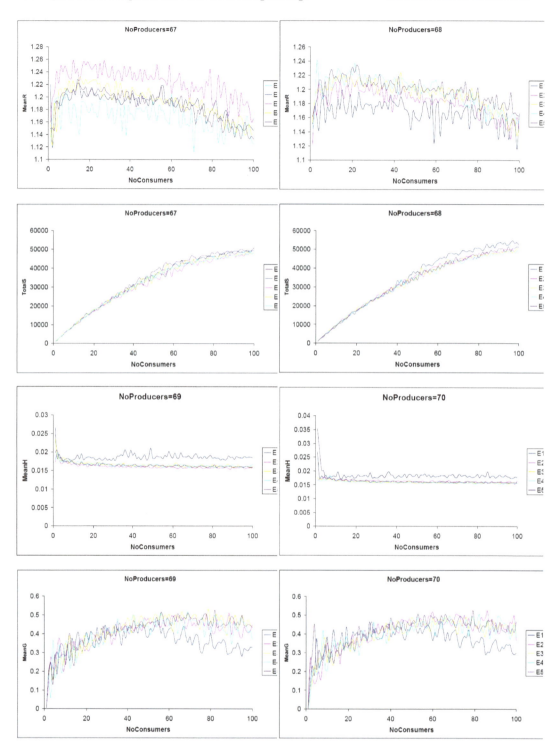

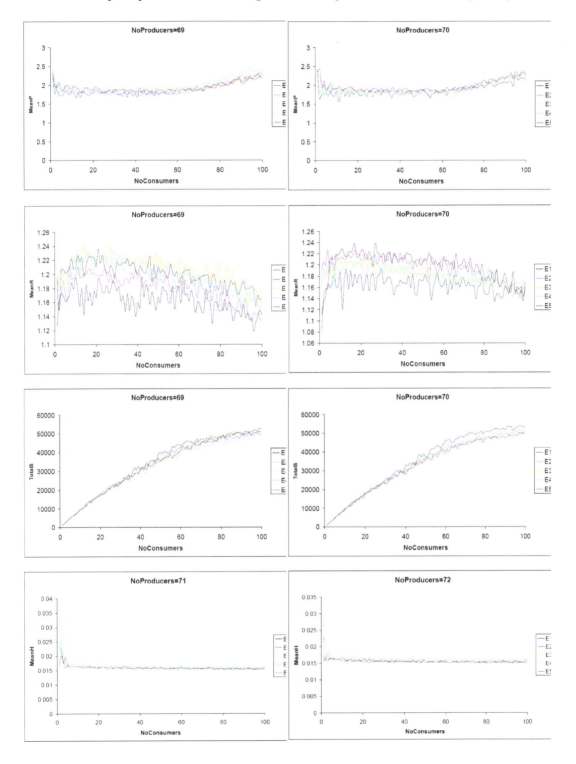

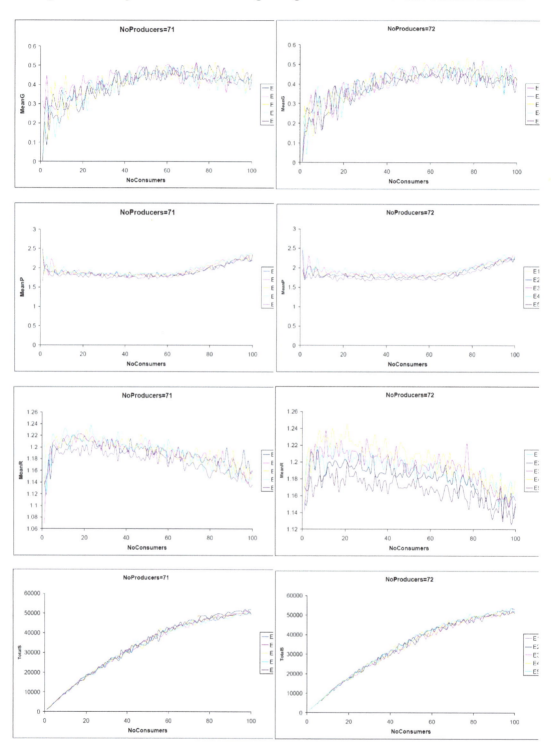

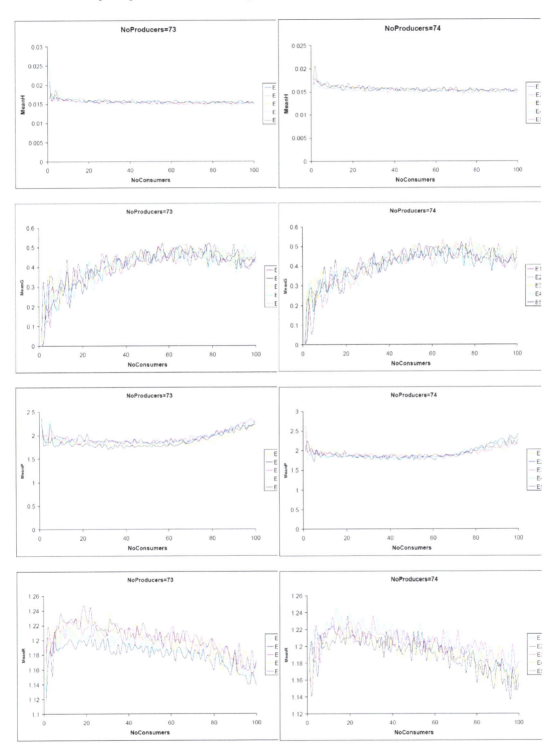

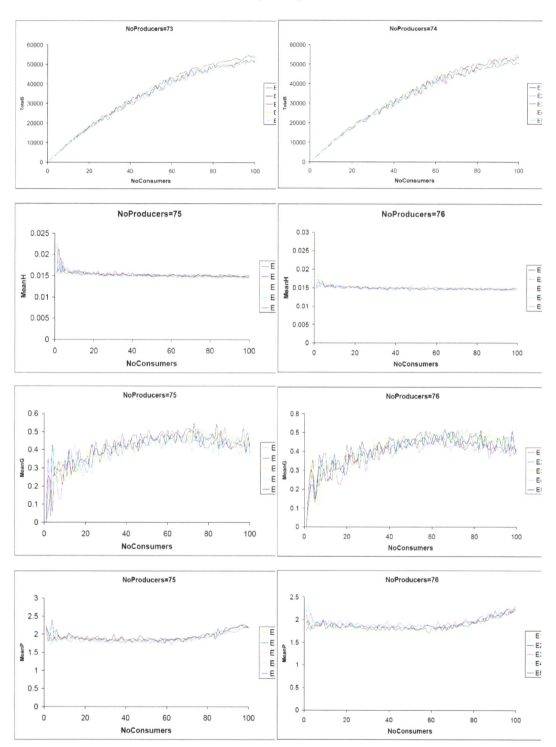

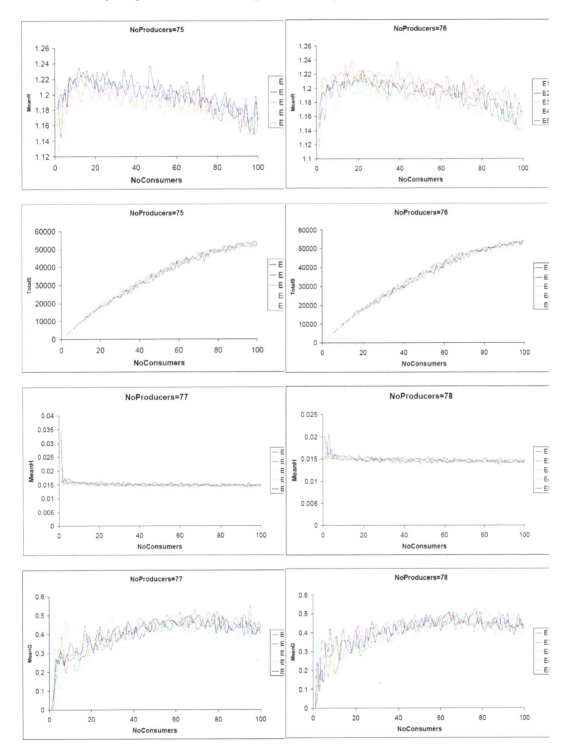

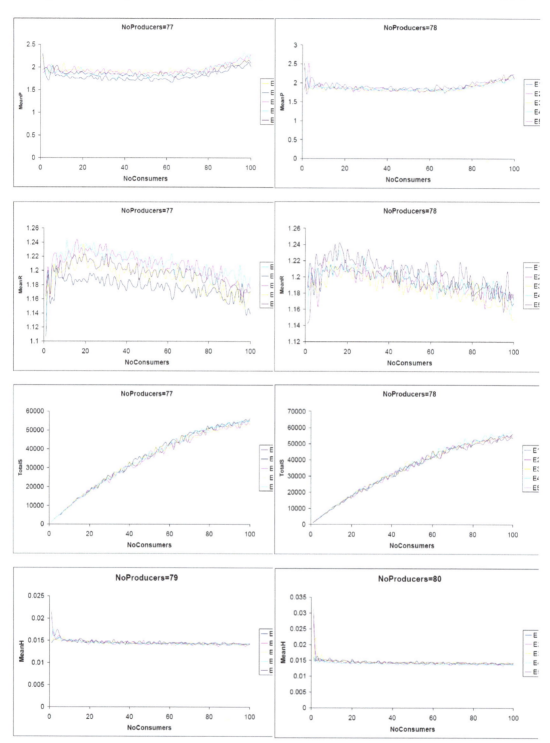

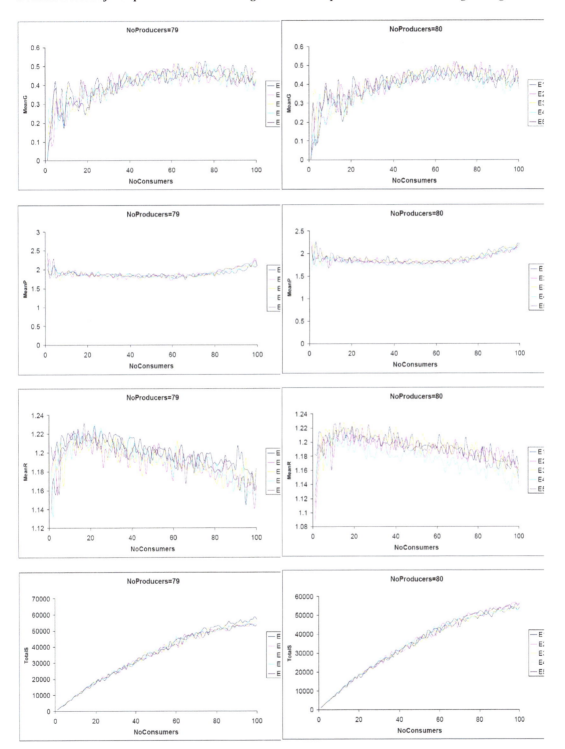

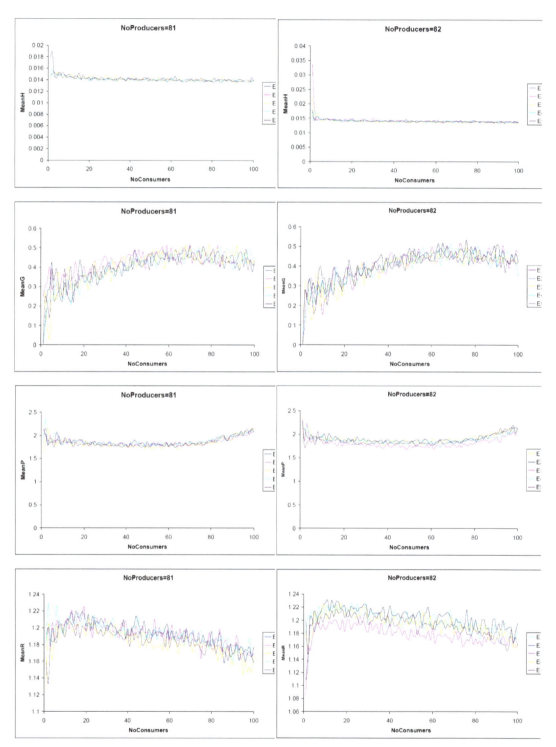

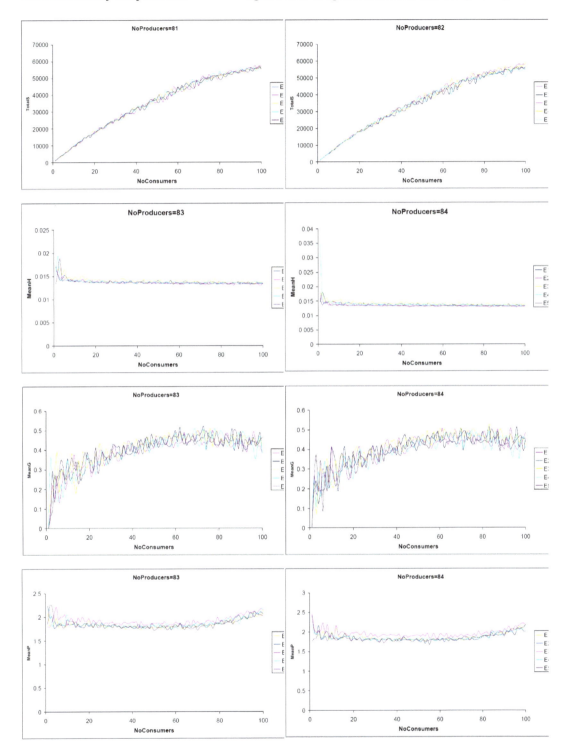

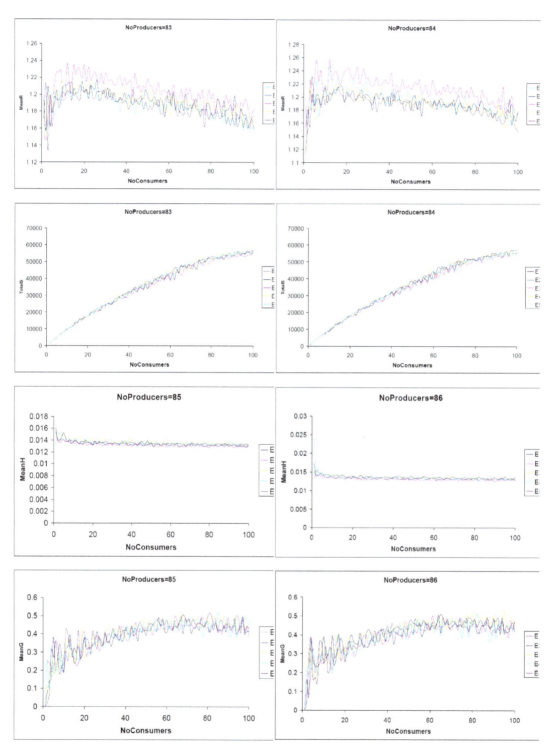

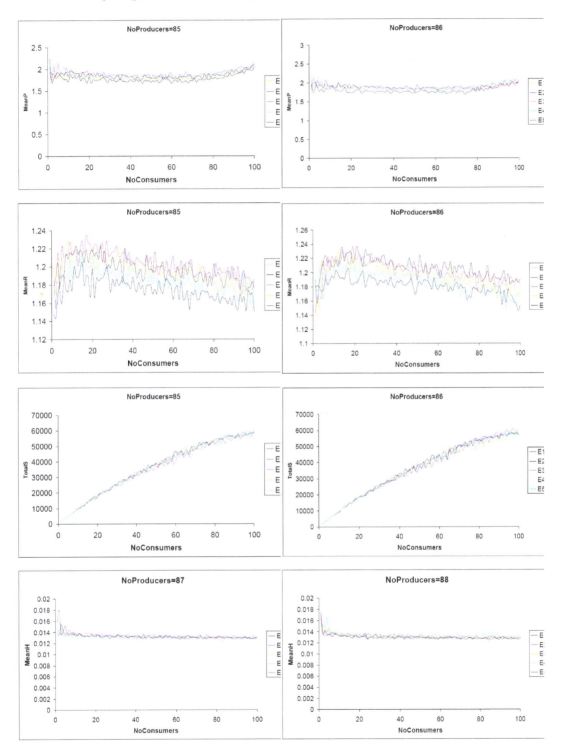

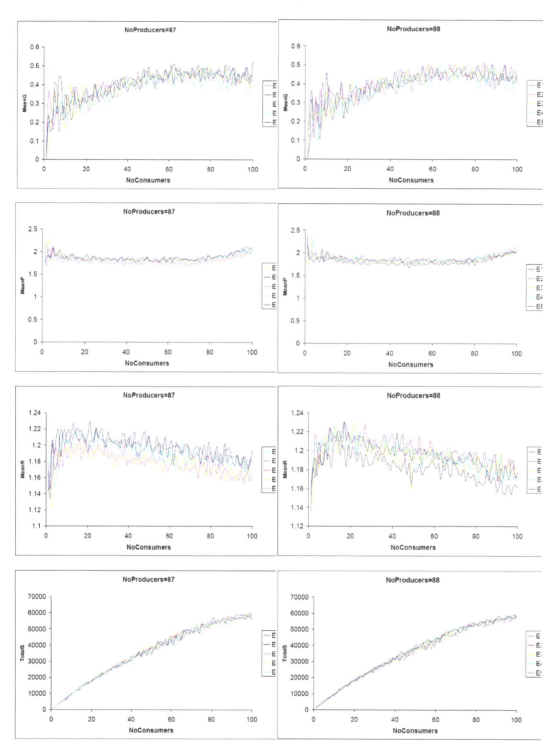

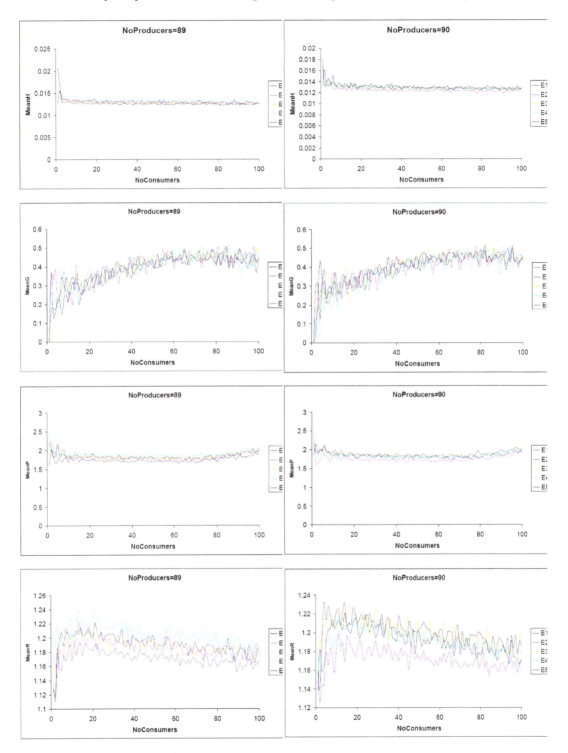

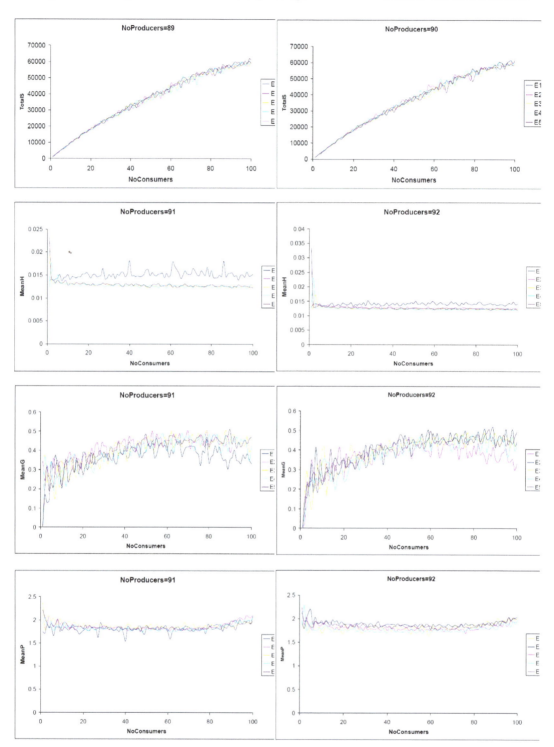

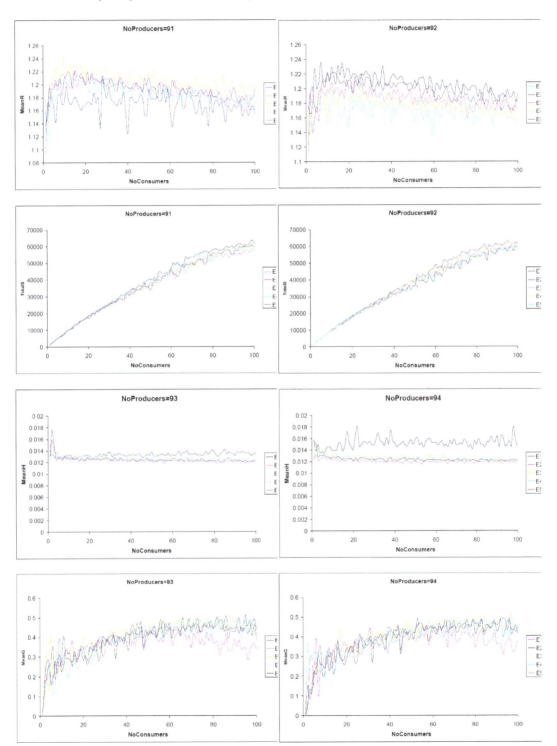

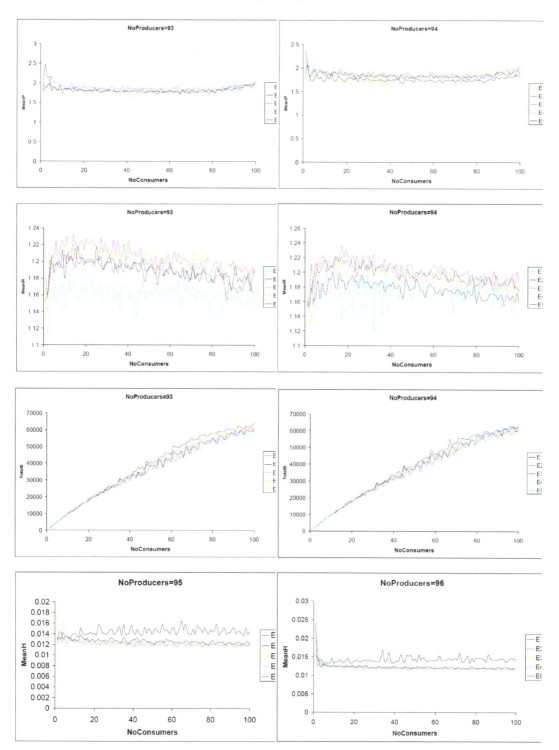

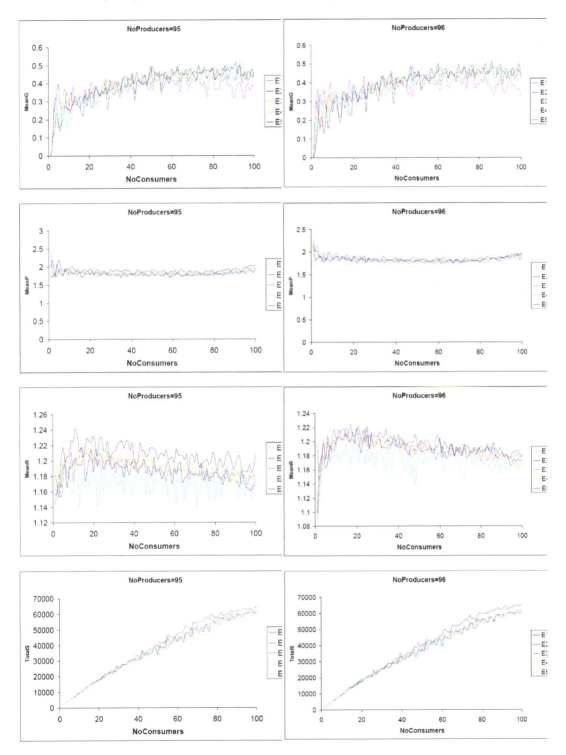

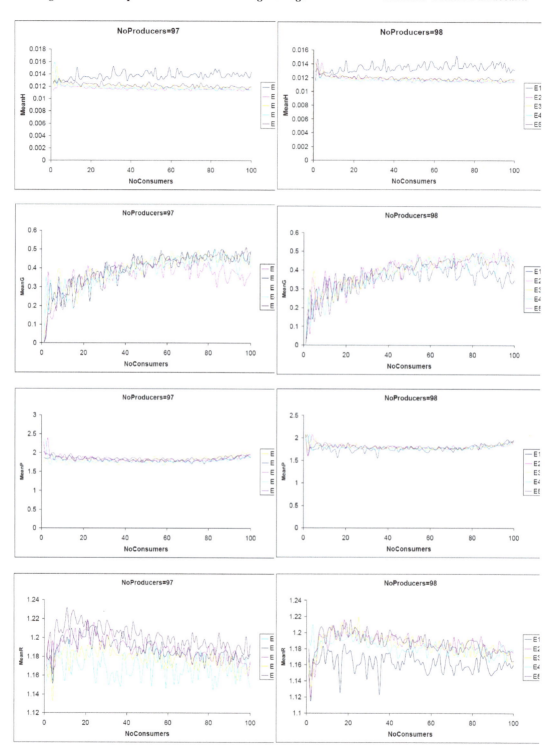

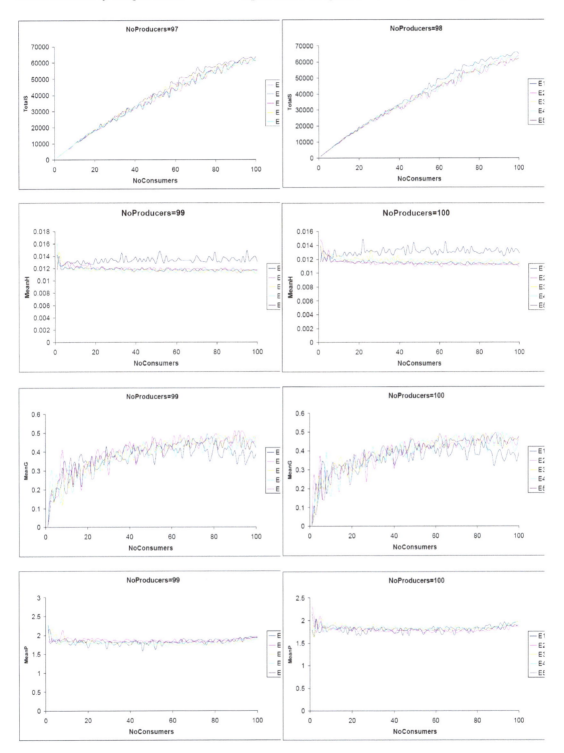

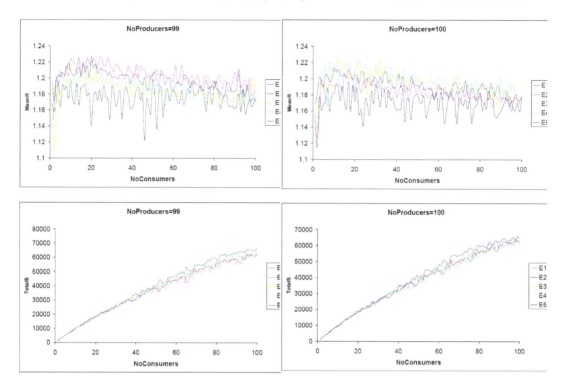

INDEX

A

Agent-based Computational Economics	3, 7
agent-based computational model	19, 20,25
Agent-based Computational Modeling	3, 4
agents	3, 4, 9, 10, 11, 13, 14,
algorithms	19, 37
Applied Computational Mathematics	3

C

catastrophe theory	5
chaos theory	5
competitiveness	83
computerized model	12
conceptual model	12, 13, 20, 37

D

dynamic equilibrium	4

E

econometrics	4
economic systems	7, 8, 9, 12

G

general theory of systems	8
Gini index	28, 48, 57, 59, 73
Global performance	83

H

Herfindahl-Hirschman index	73, 74, 78, 83

L

linear models	4